C

introduction

*all humanity is passion; without passion, religion,
history, novels, art would be ineffectual.*

honoré de balzac

have you ever wished your love life were
better—more intimate, more exciting, and
more fun? Well, there's no reason you can't make it
so, even in our hurry-up, overworked, don't-stop-and-
smell-the-roses society. Everyone needs people—
friends, lovers, and mates—who round out the rough
corners of their lives. More to the point, everyone
needs pleasure! You deserve it, so don't wait any longer
to have a happy, healthy relationship that fulfills you
spiritually, emotionally, and sexually.

Someone once said, "Approach love and cooking
with hopeless abandon." This book endeavors to do

that and much, much more! It shows you how to bring spirit and verve to all of your romantic encounters. What better way to celebrate love, passion, and magick than by getting creative, adding some spice, and heating things up to a whole new level?

Throughout history, people trusted in many things to further romance and passion—be it clothing, a gentle perfume, or special foods. *The Sexy Sorceress* shows you how to apply this vast storehouse of knowledge and lore to every aspect of your love life. You'll learn how to create ambiance using candles, costumes, aromatics, and fabulous foods—all of which are supported and enhanced by spells, charms, and rituals. The result? Hot, sexy encounters that will steam up the windows on a cold January night . . . playful pillow fights to liven up a mundane Sunday afternoon . . . or intimate walks on a moonlit evening. The choice is up to you. *The Sexy Sorceress* helps you set the energy for whatever you desire.

Speaking of desire, any sexy sorceress knows that variety is the spice of life. Whether you're heterosexual, homosexual, polyamorous, bicurious, or another interesting flavor of lover, there are simple ways to take any exercise herein and change it to suit your needs and personal lifestyle. Why does *The Sexy Sorceress* take this approach? Because magick is about connecting with the power of the natural world. Take a walk through the forest or go snorkeling in the Caribbean and you'll notice the almost endless variety of flora and fauna. If Mother Nature can hold space for such diversity, surely you can allow yourself more freedom and creativity in expressing yourself sexually. You may feel romantic and tender one night and lustfully wanton the next. Embrace it! Balance is important—even in pleasure.

One thing that *is* desperately unbalanced is the way that society has made many people feel about their bodies and sexuality. In the West, it seems that while the media inundate us daily with images of ideal beauty, there still are certain negative associations connected with being sexy, and sexually active, especially for women. While you do need to respect the sanctity of your body, and the very real health issues that arise from sexual activity, you should let go of the puritanical guilt about sex and being sexy that is hardwired into many of our mental codes. One goal of this book is to help you change your perceptions. Sensuality, by its very nature, should allow not only for what you need, but also for what you want.

You may wonder whether or not it's ethical to use magick for what you want rather than what you need. The answer to this question—most of the time—is yes. The history of magick is filled with people who had wants and used their arts to help fulfill those desires. The only real caution is to make sure that your motivations are positive, and that your wants do not harm anyone, including yourself. With that caveat concluded (and knowing that the instructions provided in this book will help you ensure that your magick does no harm), you can focus on getting in touch with your unique sexual energy. That, in and of itself, will make you more attractive to others.

To this end, *The Sexy Sorceress* begins with an exploration of the interesting and odd history of the quest for pleasure, beauty, and erotica. We're certainly not the first people who have tried to figure out what makes our potential partners tick! In some societies, in fact, pleasuring self or others became a valued art form (a perfectly legal one, by the way, for which taxes could even be levied).

The Sexy Sorceress also shows you how to create the right mood for yourself and your potential partner(s) with things like massage, aromatherapy, rituals, and, of course, the foods of love. As you read, do the following. First, let your hair down—be ready to try new things. One of the ways to break out of old molds is to explore possible new horizons. Second, start making a list of those things that you enjoy sexually and romantically, and then make time to *do them*. Don't get so caught up with day-to-day rushing that you forget to nurture passion in yourself and in your relationships.

Passion comes from inside of you; it's not predicated on having a certain amount of time, money, or the perfect body. You and your partner may have demanding schedules, financial troubles, and many other stresses that make you feel less inspired, less sexy, and less interested than you'd like to be. However, touching and caressing are great stress relievers, and even more important to engage in when times are tough. So get with your partner and consider working through this book together (and if you're single and still looking for that perfect partner, this book will make the dating game a whole lot more colorful!).

No matter what your life situation, my prayer is that these pages provide you with a little more joy, not just in the bedroom, but also in daily life.

Aphrodisiac Accounting

the history and lore of inspiring passion

When one looks at a clam on the beach, it hardly seems like something that would be associated with love. In fact, if I'd been an ancient wanderer, I'm not even sure I would have thought of trying to eat it—yet our ancestors did just that to bolster passion. Similarly, while roses smell lovely, who thought of using them to ensnare an unassuming lover? What was the first cream or oil applied to enhance attractiveness, and why? This chapter explores the many items people have used throughout the ages to ensure love, romance, and desire, as well as the folk foundations of passionate magick.

The standards of beauty and handsomeness have changed over time. Even today, what is considered attractive or sexy varies wildly among countries, cultures, and ethnic groups. Most people cannot help but be influenced by external standards of beauty, be it the models in *Vogue* or the opinions of their peer group. However, the goal of sensual sorcery is not one of playing to fads. Rather, you will use yourself and your inner spiritual compass as the starting point for rediscovering true beauty.

Historically, people have regarded beauty as something that transcends time, trends, and different cultural ideals of attractiveness. Outer beauty reflected a person's inner beauty and the essence that endured—the individual spirit. In turn, this beauty (no matter how it was defined by current fashion), had an eternal sense about it and came to symbolize something greater than the individual—the Divine potential.

This idea of beauty and its ideal was explored extensively in art, science, and literature in the hope of understanding it better. The Greek philosopher Pythagoras described beauty as being a foundation of form and structure. Pliny the Elder, a Roman scholar and naturalist, summed up his feelings about beauty by saying that expression, carriage, emotion, and intelligence all combined to create an outward manifestation of the true person. German philosopher Immanuel Kant described beauty as a universal principle that, for whatever reason, deeply affects the human heart. During the Victorian era, post-Raphaelite artists depicted the beauty of nature, and people's interaction with it. The early graphic arts in China captured not only the Chinese ideals of beauty, but also the sensual eroticism prevalent in that culture.

Over time, artists, visionaries, and great thinkers sought to define beauty in esoteric terms rather than merely depicting the physical. However, over the last several decades, an odd dichotomy has emerged in our society regarding what constitutes attractiveness. On one hand we have sayings such as "beauty is only skin deep," while on the other we have television shows such as *The Swan* that have turned plastic surgery into a kind of altar that people use to re-create themselves in the image of Ken and Barbie dolls.

People from ages twenty to eighty suffer from negative self-images. Today's teens are very uncertain about what physical ethical guidelines they're supposed to follow (should I wear a halter, can I wear my pants at the hips, can I kiss on the first date?), let alone how to feel about themselves in light of commercials that are saturated with sexy images and unattainable physiques. We've become a society that looks for drive-through cures such as shopping, plastic surgery, and endless physical adornment, rather than nurturing aspects of our beauty—such as passion, intelligence, and compassion—that will outlast the inevitable wrinkles, weight gain, and physical changes that occur over time.

The goal of this book is to help you get in touch with something longer lasting, something that begins at the roots of your self-image and works out from that space. Right now, promise to begin nurturing that seed of your Sacred Self. Be prepared to look at yourself in new ways—ways that are not shaped by culture or the media, but by the Divine nature within you. Your spirit and soul are beautiful things. They're treasures, worthy of time and attention and love and desire, no matter what the fashion magazines may say.

Meditate on the Beauty Within

This meditation requires about 30 to 40 minutes of private time. The purpose of this activity is to rediscover the sacred spark of your true being and begin fanning that flame into a bright, vibrant light. First, get comfortable. You can sit or stand for this visualization, but make sure that your clothing and environment make you feel completely at ease. The fewer distractions there are, the better your results will be.

Stretch a bit before you begin. This helps the relaxation process. Close your eyes and breathe deeply, in through your nose and out through your mouth. Focus only on the sound of your heartbeat and every breath you take. Focus on these while remaining aware of and connected to all the sensations that are running through your body.

Once you feel centered, and as if the world's distractions are very far away, direct your attention to the region of your heart. This is typically where people think of their soul and spirit abiding, so it's the natural place to seek the sacred spark. At first, see only your physical self as you are right now, looking keenly at the area around your heart. Now imagine that your eyesight is like a movie camera, and slowly zoom in. In this spiritual space you can go beyond the surface of your skin—you can go within.

At first it may seem dark, but continue to focus on the comforting company of your heartbeat and breathing. They are your constant guides and guardians here. Slow, steady . . . sure. Wait in the darkness. Let its peace and quiet envelop you, like a soft down comforter on a cold winter night. Now, cast your inner eyes in different directions. Be patient. You aren't used to seeing things this way, and most people find it takes more than one try to be successful.

What should you look for in this activity? Though everyone's experience will be a little different, you're looking for a glow, a warmth, or something familiar and welcoming. The color, size, and shape of these things are unique for each person (note these mentally, so you can look them up in symbol books later to understand a little more of where you are in terms of your spiritual progress). This is the seed of your soul. It bears the fingerprint of who you are and who you've been in every incarnation. It is also incredibly beautiful—it is the true *you*.

Now try an experiment. As you look at that glowing spark, focus on directing white-light energy toward it. If it helps, see the light pouring down through your physical head and out through your physical hands toward the spiritual presence. You're doing this activity correctly when you see the spark grow (and in some cases change color or shape). That transformation is due to the care and feeding you're giving to your spirit.

At this juncture, you can begin to back out your internal camera and return to normal awareness. Write down your impressions in a notebook or journal. Also, pay particular attention to how this activity changes your perceptions of yourself, others, and your environment. The changes in your perceptions or emotions will be subtle at first, but the more often you take time to energize your Sacred Self, the more pronounced the changes will become.

Savory Sensuality and Edible Adoration

Mind, body, and spirit are intimately connected. It's difficult to feel passionate, for example, when you're ill or tired. Once humankind made that initial realization, the next natural step was finding ways to nourish the body so that the "heart" would be encouraged toward warm, loving, or passionate feelings. If food wasn't available, aromatics were another handy choice. That's hardly surprising, given how intricately linked our sense of taste and smell are. Incense, oils, and other scented items have been utilized in sacred practices for thousands of years, either to fragrance the body or to add enticing aroma to food and drink. And, as with most things used in religion, aromatics found their way into magick and into daily life.

With this history in mind, this section examines edibles and aromatics, where they were used, and by whom and how. I've eliminated things that are unsavory or impractical to the modern magickal home, and focused on those things that you can easily buy, if they're not already part of your pantry. This is an excellent starting point for your sensual sorcery adventures. Let your senses be your guides.

Aioli

A French sauce made with garlic, egg, and olive oil, known for its ability to improve sexual interest. Serve this over green vegetables such as asparagus. Aioli can be found at gourmet shops, or made at home by whipping an egg with garlic and olive oil, and pouring it over the asparagus just a few minutes before it is done cooking.

Almond

Throughout the ancient world, the almond tree stood as a symbol of fertility and love, and the nuts were used in candy form as a common wedding favor. Romans even went so far as to present newlyweds with a bundle of almonds to insure fertility. The Old Testament speaks of Aaron's rod bearing almonds; in India, people ate these nuts to sustain mental and physical prowess. Try some almond incense to arouse passion in your female lovers, or serve some almond-paste candies (marzipan) as a special after-dinner-before-bed treat.

Anise

The Greeks, Romans, and Egyptians all used anise as an aphrodisiac, the Greeks and Romans in particular. The Egyptians also considered it a valuable digestive aid. Anise seed's reputation didn't wane over time. Medieval Europeans continued to use anise seed in love potions. As a woman's herb, anise has constituents and effects similar to estrogen. Drink some daily to stay young and vibrant! A nice side benefit, of course, is that the seeds also make your mouth fresh and kissable.

Apricot

The Chinese tell us that apricots represent the sensual part of human nature. Throughout the Far East, these beautiful little fruits gained the folk title of "moon of the faithful." It seems the Latin-speaking countries agreed with the value of apricots, giving them the name *praecocia*, which translates as "precious." The Greeks and Romans believed that apricot nectar was tasty enough to please even the gods.

Artichoke

The folklore of Elizabethan times says this vegetable was once a beautiful woman who made the gods angry. The Roman naturalist Pliny felt it a very valuable addition to the kitchen and medicinal garden. Typically, artichoke was recommended for men who felt their libido failing.

Arugula

This herb, which bears the folk name "rocket seed," has been used as an aphrodisiac since about the first century c.e. The piquant flavor seems to heat up one's body. Love experts recommend that for best results, arugula should be added to parsnips, pine nuts, orchid bulbs, or pistachios. When arugula is used in pasta or salad, the addition of nuts in particular will increase a male partner's potency so he can last the night.

Asparagus

Romans cultivated asparagus very early in history, enjoying it both in fresh and dried form. The phallic appearance of this vegetable made it perfectly suited to improving male fertility and longevity. A love manual from sixteenth-century Arabia specifically recommends asparagus for improving a man's desire. In the eighteenth century, Madame de Pompadour regularly added it to her passion-inducing blends; the nineteenth century found Frenchmen trusting in asparagus to improve their bedroom prowess, and they often ate it before the wedding night. Recent studies indicate that the vitamins in asparagus can improve hormone production.

Avocado

The Aztec language named this tree *Ahuacatl*, which translates as "testicle." In looking at this plant, it's easy to see why such an association came about—the fruit naturally hangs in pairs. Therefore, as dictated by the law of similars, avocados were used in medical or folkloric treatment of the male parts. This association remained in popular fashion well into the twenty-first century, helped in part by the lush texture of the fruit. Try some sliced with a zesty vinegar, salt, and pepper.

Banana

Buddhist texts dating to 600 B.C.E. mention bananas. The flower of this fruit looks very phallic, as does the fruit itself, which is why it became a popular aphrodisiac, especially in Polynesian regions. It's interesting to note that Islamic stories claim that Adam and Eve covered themselves with banana leaves instead of fig leaves! Practically speaking, bananas provide both vitamin B and potassium, both of which are known to help with hormone production.

Basil (sweet)

A rather humorous legend instructs that if one is to grow potent basil, one should swear and rant while planting. Greeks trusted in this herb to improve both fertility and a person's sex drive, and Italian women wore basil to indicate their availability and interest. Indian tradition holds the herb as sacred to Vishnu, whose wife transformed into basil on earth. It continues to be a common component in love potions.

Beef

The natural amino acids and protein in beef will help keep you alert and strong through a long night of making love. Just be careful, because if you have too much meat it can cause indigestion and completely dispel any benefits gained.

Cardamom

Traditional Indian herbal books say that mixing this herb with honey and warm milk will cure impotence in a man and help him avoid premature orgasms.

Carrot

As with bananas, the shape of a carrot gave it an association with men's virility. It's interesting to discover that the ancient carrot, which has a 35-million-year history, once came in many colors, including yellow, red, green, and purple! The Greeks instructed men to eat carrots for tenacity, and women to consume them for acquiescence. They also believed that drinking carrot juice improved a woman's chance of conception. The Roman emperor Caligula ate large amounts of this vegetable, believing it to be very helpful to his lovemaking powers.

Caviar

Around the world people regard caviar as a rare delicacy. Because caviar is fish roe—eggs—it is associated with fertility, especially for women.

Celery

According to Swedish lore, people who eat celery will find themselves aroused. Women in ancient Rome ate celery to increase their desire, and Madame de Pompadour served celery soup regularly for similar reasons. Some studies indicate that eating a lot of celery apparently produces some bodily aromas that naturally attract women.

Chocolate

Chocolate, which the Aztecs considered sacred, seems to have originated in the region of Mexico where their civilization flourished. It was regularly a part of engagements as a tasty treat for guests and weddings, as well as a seemly offering for the gods. Modern studies show that chocolate contains chemicals that excite pleasure centers, especially for women, and chemically it has more antioxidants than does red wine.

Cloves

Romans used cloves, another "hot" food, to help in matters of the heart, especially to inspire love.

Coffee

Folklore credits an unsuspecting Ethiopian shepherd with discovering coffee. Apparently he nibbled on some berries and suddenly found himself able to stay awake all night. A monk wandering by thought the man was drunk, but after some conversation he too discovered the coffee bean's benefits (it helped him stay awake through his prayers and meditations). The energizing effect is why coffee was added to the lists of aphrodisiac food—it helps us make love until dawn.

Coriander

Also known as cilantro seed, coriander thrived in the Hanging Gardens of Babylon. The ancient Chinese used it in love potions regularly, while Arabian stories claim that a potion of coriander cured a couple that had remained childless for forty years!

Cucumber

The shape of cucumbers made it an ideal phallic symbol. Recent research done in Chicago indicates that the aroma of cucumbers has the potential of arousing some women.

Fig

Greeks and Romans alike used figs in art to represent fertility. In that region it's believed that the goddess Demeter created the fruit and gave it to humans. Lore tells us that breaking open a fig in front of your lover causes arousal, perhaps because the open fig looks like female sex organs.

Garlic

Sanskrit writings speak of garlic as having a heating effect that stirs sexual desires. This idea was later reflected in Middle Eastern folklore that claims garlic keeps a person strong and brave. Because of this reputation, Egyptians fed garlic to workers and warriors alike. If you plan to give some to your lover, either have plenty yourself or keep a good helping of breath mints handy!

Ginger

Ginger naturally stimulates circulation. In the wild, it takes on a bumpy, hornlike appearance, which may have lead to its designation as "horn root" in

Sanskrit. Arabian books say that ginger gives men so much energy that both he and his partner will experience immeasurable pleasure!

Honey

Honey was listed in the Egyptian pharmaceuticals as a cure for sterility. The Romans also considered it valuable enough to offer it to deities and used it to pay taxes. During the Middle Ages, honey was a common addition to wine for the wedding night (mead) so that the couple would have a sweet, fertile union.

Licorice

Licorice is actually sweeter than sugar in its natural form, which is how it got the folk name of sweet root. Egyptians placed pieces of licorice in King Tut's tomb, considering it a cure-all even in the afterlife! If you chew on licorice it improves lust, especially in women. If you don't have licorice, however, fennel's similarity in flavor makes an ideal substitute.

Mango

There's a lovely Hindu story that talks of a mango tree that sprouted from the ashes of the Sun Princess. The Emperor adored the beauty of mango flowers and the flavor of the fruit and came to enjoy it all the time. When the first fruit of this particular tree ripened, it landed at the Emperor's feet and released the Princess.

Since that day, mangos have remained an emblem of love and friendship.

Mead

Many cultures believed that mead, an ancient fermented beverage with honey for sweetener, was a divine gift. Celtic families always gave a hefty portion to newlyweds (see also Honey, this chapter), enough to last a full month. This tradition resulted in the term "honeymoon" as the post-wedding celebratory time. In addition to having aphrodisiac qualities, mead also provides inspiration, bravery, and wisdom.

Mustard

German brides attached mustard seeds to their wedding dresses. By custom this ensured that the bride would be a strong mistress in her household. Some folkways instruct that placing mustard around the house keeps everyone therein safe (and it's a good way to keep unwanted visitors away during your private moments). Danish cures for frigidity include mustard seed, and the Chinese use it to promote desire.

Nutmeg

Chinese women so prized this spice that they would pay as much as three sheep and a cow for a small amount. Greeks, Romans, and Arabs likewise treasured it for prolonging lovemaking, especially when mixed with egg and honey.

Onion

Egyptian priests abstained from onions for fear that eating them would create uncontrollable lust. Hindu and Arabic books recommended them for passion, and in France newlyweds ate onion soup during their honeymoon to improve sexual interest and overall energy levels.

Oysters

Aphrodite, the goddess of love and beauty, was born from a living sea on the shell of an oyster. As if that didn't give this food's reputation enough of a kick-start, legends claim that Casanova ate fifty oysters daily (often off the breasts of a beautiful woman). Romans documented oysters as aphrodisiacs, sometimes in amusing ways. A satire by Juvenal describes various woman letting loose sexually after eating giant oysters with wine. Modern science shows us that the zinc level in oysters can help male sperm production.

Peach

The Chinese consider peaches the fruit of immortality and sexual well-being. A person who eats of God's peach tree in the afterlife will receive virility and eternal youth. Japanese lore, meanwhile, tells of a child who was born from a peach tree and whose parents showed him endless love and devotion. This gave him the strength to become a great hero; consequently, the peach remained a symbol of sagacity and emotional devotion, no matter the circumstances.

Pepper

The Perfumed Garden, an Arabic love guide, suggests using pepper mixed with ginger, honey, and lavender to inspire a man's interest. Indian custom instructs similarly, except it uses pepper with almonds and milk. In both situations, the hot nature of pepper is likely the reason for the symbolism.

Pine Nuts

In Greece and Rome, pine nuts were eaten with honey to stimulate sexual energy. Ovid lists them as aphrodisiacs, as did an Arabic book of love advice. Reputedly, eating 100 of them mixed with honey for three nights is very restorative! Druids used them for fertility magick too. Like oysters, pine nuts have a high zinc level that may improve male potency.

Pineapple

Called an excellent fruit in the Caribbean, native peoples kept pineapples (or depictions of pineapples) all around the house as a sign of friendship and welcome to travelers. This motif showed up again in Victorian

America, where pineapple was used as a homeopathic cure for impotence.

Pomegranate

One of the most valued physical relationship tomes, the Kamasutra, recommends this fruit as passion's helpmate. The number of seeds in the fruit represented fertility and abundance in numerous ancient cultures, including those of the Hebrews, Greeks, and Berbers. Berber women used pomegranate to divine how many children they would conceive. Chinese wedding guests received sugared pomegranate seeds and gave them to the newly married couple to bring them great happiness and fertility.

Quince

Quince fruit was associated with Venus and Aphrodite, the goddesses of love and beauty in Roman and Greek mythology. Perhaps this is why some legends claim that the true fruit of temptation in Eden was actually the quince! In any case, the Greeks and Romans used the fruit as part of the wedding ritual. Both the bride and the groom would eat from the same quince to link their lives in joy and ensure them many children.

Rice

In parts of Asia, eating from the same rice bowl as a person of the opposite sex acts as a declaration of engagement. In those regions, as in the Western world, wedding guests tossed rice at the bride and groom to bring them good luck and fertility. Similarly, in Rajasthan, a woman entering her husband's home after the wedding scattered rice on the threshold to bring joy and abundance.

Roses

Roses are edible, giving them a lot of flexibility for your sensual sorcery. Throughout history, roses were used in love potions and as gifts between lovers. In fact, Anthony and Cleopatra were said to woo each other in a room where the floor was strewn with rose petals. Persians stuffed the sultan's mattress with rose petals (which probably pleased his wives, too!). Emperors in Rome filled their baths with rose water and surrounded themselves with abundant fragrant petals during orgies.

The popularity of roses reached an impressive height during the Victorian era, when each color of rose had special symbolic meaning. The red rose symbolized love, respect, and courage. White roses spoke of purity, worth, and beauty. Pink roses represented grace, sympathy, and admiration. Yellow was equated with joy and friendship, coral with desire, burgundy with gentle beauty, and rosebuds with innocent or young love.

Saffron

Folklore claims that saffron makes all of your favorite erogenous zones even more sensitive. That may be why the Greeks and Romans added this spice to bath water. According to regional myths, a mortal named Crocos fell in love with a nymph, Smilax. When Smilax denied him, he turned into the plant from which saffron is harvested, *Crocus sativus*.

Sake

The Japanese use sake at wedding rituals as a symbol of fertility. Both the bride and groom take nine sips of this beverage to make their union official.

Strawberries

Share a double strawberry with another if you wish to fall in love with him or her! These wonderful fruits are sacred to Venus, the Roman goddess of beauty and adoration. In the immortal words of the seventeenth-century English writer William Butler, "God could have made a better berry, but doubtless God never did."

Sweet Potato

Sixteenth-century herbals and love manuals instruct the reader to eat sweet potato tarts to kick-start passion.

Truffle

The ancients often felt that the more rare or expensive something was, the better it worked magickally. Truffles fall into this category. Jean Anthelme Brillat-Savarin, an eighteenth-century writer, is quoted as saying that people of that era believed truffles excited "the genetic sense." They continue to be regarded as an affection-producing food.

Vanilla

Vanilla's aroma is said to improve a person's lust and overall pleasure. While it's uncertain how this spice gained that reputation, a Mexican story may give us a clue. It speaks of a Mexican fertility goddess, Xanat, who desperately loved a young man. When she found out she could not marry him because she was Divine, she changed herself into the vanilla plant to provide him joy and pleasure all the days of his life.

Walnut

People in France and Italy once ate walnuts to improve desire. Romans tossed walnut pieces at newlyweds much as other cultures used rice to symbolize fertility.

Wine

I think that the immortal words of Omar Khayyám (a Persian poet) express the wonder of wine perfectly: "A flask of wine, a book of verse, and thou!"

This chapter has been but a short exploration of the ways in which our ancestors tried to encourage love and passion. As you can see, there weren't many stones left unturned. The key is finding ways to apply this knowledge in a modern setting effectively and sensitively. So let's move on and examine creating just the right setting and mood for your sensual sorcery.

nothing great in the world has ever been accomplished without passion.

georg wilhelm friedrich hegel

2

Courting

creating just the right mood

n o matter how great the aphrodisiac, ambiance counts for a lot in creating just the right space in which your passions can play themselves out perfectly. Where should you begin? We'll talk more about your personal preparations in the next chapter. First, however, you should focus on making your loving space as welcoming and reflective of your goals as possible, not just visually and physically, but spiritually too.

The first step is to think creatively about your space and what it can offer to you metaphysically. Your home or apartment is about to become a different space—one that is infused with the intent and energy of seduction. Rather than just a place where you hang your hat, it's the oven in which you cook up your sensual sorcery (which gives whole new meaning to heating things up!). However, to accomplish this, you need to look at your home space with your spiritual eyes. Rediscover the magickal potential in the loving space around you, and carry that expectant attitude with you throughout your preparations. Remember, attitude and willpower drive successful spells.

Hand-in-hand with that expectant eye, ask yourself if the space can be adapted to a theme. Think about transforming your home into a special fantasy. For example, a few drapes hung around the ceiling in an ordinary living room and some well-placed candles change that plain space into an Arabic oasis. Or, some fresh flowers, fruits, an ocean CD, and rich aromatics make your bedroom a tropical paradise!

The options are as endless as your imagination will allow. Better still, this type of decoration gives you a starting point for pondering foods, beverages, and clothing for your tryst. You can also often find most, if not all, of what you need right around your own home.

Third, do a little cleanup. A lot of dirt or clutter is very distracting. Besides, you don't want the object of your seduction staring at the green bean under the refrigerator as you make love on the kitchen floor. That doesn't mean you have to transform your home into something pristine enough for a magazine cover. You still want both you and your partner to be comfortable. So think of what your normal sense of "clean" requires and go that route. After that, a few pillows tossed here and there or a magazine and coaster provide a more relaxed feeling without taking away the neatness. Dim lighting will set the mood and hide anything you didn't have time to get to.

Besides having a space that makes you proud, there are numerous advantages to this brief bit of primping. From a metaphysical standpoint (also see Feng Shui Fantasies later in this chapter) clutter and dirt hinder

activity • memory moods

When you have about 30 or 45 minutes, take a walk through the place in which you plan to have your passionate encounter. Think about the various experiences or scenarios that tend to put both you and your mate in the right mood. Next, consider what you have on hand that could help re-create that ambiance. Remember, this doesn't have to be a remodeling project—you're just nudging a memory or feeling to the surface with subtle, symbolic, and meaningful touches. You may not be able to literally go to Paris, but filling the room with candles, twinkling lights, and champagne bottles will evoke the feeling of a romantic evening in the City of Lights. Write down your ideas and use them as the starting point for playfully assembling some decorations. Also keep these items in mind when you're reviewing the aromas and colors discussed in this chapter, the smooth flow of energy, not to mention causing stress. So focus on your goals and use the activity of tidying up as a foundation for all the magick that follows. As you clear away dust and stuff you don't need right now, visualize yourself discarding any old emotional baggage between you and your partner. From a more mundane viewpoint, if things get really wild, there's less potential for tripping and breakage in a clean space. It will also make your after-date cleanup process much quicker, so you can catch a much-needed nap!

Finally, if you're thinking about setting formal sacred space around your lovemaking area, or the entire living quarters, neatness seems to help. Neatness allows a smoother flow of energy; after all, have you ever seen a messy church? While there's nothing religious (per se) about what you're doing, there is something spiritual taking place—the mingling of two people's energies in an area pre-prepared for the most wonderful results possible.

Magickal and Sensual Spaces

For those of you unfamiliar with the idea of creating sacred space, think of creating a bubble of energy that's protective and all-surrounding. Whatever you want to stay within that bubble will stay. What you don't want to allow in remains firmly outside. In magickal circles, people utilize the advantage of sacred space, not only for protection, but also as a collection mechanism. When the energy in the bubble has risen to perfection, they can then direct the whole bubble toward a specific goal or need. So can you! One piece of advice: let your partner know about what you're doing, what it means, and why. He or she also needs to be comfortable with this idea for it to work properly.

Activity: Creating Sacred Space

The traditional sacred space in Neo-Pagan traditions begins with a circle that has four major points (the four directions). These four directions also represent elemental energy (north—earth; east—air; south—fire; and west—water). When building the space, the practitioner invites those elemental energies into the space, not simply to protect, but to infuse the space with their attributes to help achieve the goal. Thus, the wording of the invitation (or invocation) is specifically designed to declare those goals. Here is an example of what might be said at each of the four directional points of your sacred sexuality circle as you walk clockwise (positive energy) around it:

> *I stand in the east and welcome the powers of air*
> *Come with warmth, come with winds fair*
> *Protect and energize this space I'm in*
> *So loving communication takes place within*

I stand in the south and welcome the powers of fire
Come with passion, let our energy burn higher
Protect and energize this space I'm in
With the light of Spirit, the magick begins

I stand in the west and welcome the powers of water
Come with understanding, in our hearts stir
Protect and energize this space I'm in
With what was, what is, what will be again

I stand in the north and welcome the powers of earth
Come with grounding in which our love finds birth
Protect and energize this sacred space
All while we remain within this place
So be it.

As you move, visualize a white-gold light that connects each point to the other. From that perimeter, visualize a complete bubble of good vibrations—above your head, below your feet, and all around. You may notice that it seems quieter within, or that it's warmer somehow. That's a good indication that the invocation has worked.

Note that later on (or the next day) you'll want to thank the Powers and bid them farewell. You can do this in any way that's comfortable for you, or just adapt the invocation in reverse so you open the doorway (the bubble).

Aromatic Adoration

Whether or not you've decided to go with a theme, aromas are another subtle dimension you can add to your sensual sorcery.

Scent speaks volumes without uttering one word. The art of aromatherapy has been around for about 6,000 years, probably starting in China, where various aromatic plants were used to foster well-being. Egyptians, Greeks, and Romans also had scented oils that were recommended for everything from healing to inspiring adoration.

Modern aromatherapy came back into public awareness as a therapeutic aid in the 1930s, thanks to the French chemist Rene Maurice Gattefosse. His work was built on by others and continues to be foundational to the practice of aromatherapy today.

Aromatherapy is based on the knowledge that smell is the most primitive of human senses, and that aromas directly affect the limbic system of the brain (the part of the brain that seems to be responsible for our emotional life and the formation of memories), thereby creating various biochemical reactions in the body. Combine that with the knowledge that pheromones affect our sexual attraction levels, and it's not surprising that the use of various scents should be part of the well-rounded sensual sorcery kit. Here are some ideas to get you started.

Single Scents

In buying aromatics it is better to use essential oils and natural aromatics rather than other options, because the natural oils have a more pure vibrational signature with which to work. One caution: If you're using an essential oil in a blend that goes on your skin, test for allergies first. Also make sure your significant other is not allergic to any aromatic you plan to use.

+ *Ginger (for attracting a man):* a high-energy herb that improves overall alertness and focus
* *Jasmine (for attracting a man):* a sacred fairy flower; promotes playfulness, luck in love, and sensual openness
+ *Lavender (for attracting a man):* provides a sense of peace and comfort to help ease precoital jitters
+ *Mango:* fires up the furnace of passion, and it's also said to have wish-fulfilling properties
+ *Musk:* a traditional fragrance in sexy perfumes; used to bring out the animal nature
* *Neroli:* brings out one's sensitive nature without worry or building walls
+ *Passion fruit:* known for manifesting fantasies, and, of course, passion
+ *Patchouli (for attracting a woman):* enhances attractiveness and charisma

- *Vetivert (for attracting a woman):* inspires gentle, loving feelings, and the ability to transform with the situation(s) at hand
- *Ylang-ylang:* draws attention to the wearer by promoting confidence; also helps to soothe relationship problems by balancing auric energies between two people. Think of the aura like an envelope of energy that emanates from your body. It provides a subtle signal of how you're feeling, what you're thinking, etc., through those energy patterns.
- *Violet (for attracting a woman):* deepens friendship and overall good feelings, and improves luck

Blends

In blending aromatics, the best practice is to use no more than three, and add them a little at a time until you're happy with the balance. If you're mixing them with a base, make sure to blend thoroughly after each addition and check the final scent, adjusting accordingly.

- *Attractiveness:* lavender, mint, thyme, rosemary
- *Communication:* bergamot, anise, mint, almond, pine
- *Soothing anger:* lemon, sage, frankincense, myrrh, sandalwood
- *Love (gentle):* rose, clove, ginger, apple
- *Erotic energy:* allspice, orange, vanilla, patchouli, vetivert

+ *Celebrating feminine energy:* cedar, violet, rose, cinnamon
+ *Celebrating masculine energy:* bay, patchouli, musk, amber, clove
+ *Romantic energy:* lemon rind, orange, vanilla, rose

By the way, the energy you're using to whip up great aromatic blends can also be used to whip up some accompanying charms and spells. What you want to do here is match the purpose of the oil (love, romance, and so on) with the words of your incantation.

When practicable, use magickal timing to support your efforts, such as making the aromatic during a full moon for feminine energy, or when the sun is high in the sky for masculine energy. Repeat your incantation throughout the blending process, allowing your voice to rise naturally (this creates a cone of power that blesses your efforts). Here are some examples of incantations for the blends:

Attractiveness: "See the Inner me, my beauty and my worth; by this spell and my will I give this magick birth!"

Communication: "Communication is what I seek, bless each thought and the words I speak!"

Soothing anger: "Cool my ire, cool my rage; turn negativity into the wisdom of a sage!"

Love (gentle): "Heart open as these words are spoken. This love I freely give, in my heart love shall live."

Erotic energy: "Sexy, sensual, sensuous ME, within and without—as I will, so shall I be!"

Celebrating feminine energy: "Goddess above, goddess below—the ancient goddess I would to know. Goddess without, goddess within—let this magick now begin."

Celebrating masculine energy: "Lord of Fire, God of sun, dwell with me, let us become as one!"

Romantic energy: "Dreamy and loving spirit of romance, come and play here, with me dance!"

Astrological Aromas

Just as every sign of the zodiac has certain personality traits associated with it, each sign also has fragrances that are particular to it. Find out your mate's sign and then scent the room, or yourself, using the aromatics in the following list. You'll notice that some of the aromas listed are herb or spice based. Consider planning a seductive dinner that includes the aromas and flavors that are associated with your beloved's sign.

+ *Aries:* ginger, orange, jasmine, geranium, cinnamon
+ *Taurus:* pine, ylang-ylang, apple, patchouli, mint

- *Gemini:* sandalwood, juniper, lavender, violet, rose
- *Cancer:* myrrh, fennel, lemon, clove, camphor
- *Leo:* angelica, cedar, neroli, frankincense, musk
- *Virgo:* lemongrass, marjoram, wintergreen, narcissus
- *Libra:* sage, cherry, chamomile, acacia, lily of the valley
- *Scorpio:* basil, nutmeg, banana, civet, vetivert
- *Sagittarius:* carnation, bergamot, rosemary, coriander
- *Capricorn:* peppermint, thyme, musk, wisteria
- *Aquarius:* clove, rose, patchouli, vervain, jasmine
- *Pisces:* lemon, nutmeg, vanilla, lavender, ambergris

By the way, don't use any scent to which your partner might be allergic, or one that may bring up a sad or bad memory. Aromatics can bring a lot of emotions to bear, so trust your instincts and use this list as a generalized guideline only.

Now you might be wondering how you can put all this information to use. Whether you go for one well-chosen scent or a blend, you can find numerous ways to apply these ideas. Consider the following ways to work a little sexy scent into the atmosphere:

- Air fresheners
- Carpet fresheners
- Making a personal perfume or cologne based in oil or alcohol
- Scented candles

- Mouthwash (for a kissable nature)
- An aromatherapy bath for one . . . or better, two!
- Decorative potpourri (fresh or dried—but fresh is more potent)
- Creams (add your chosen scent to unscented cream) or massage oil
- Body powder (add finely powdered herbs to an unscented base)
- Scented soap (find the aroma you need and treat your mate to a seductive shower)
- Incense (make your own or buy what you need)
- Floral arrangements (hey, say it with flowers!)

Remember to tie your choices into your chosen decorating scheme.

It's a testament to the power of scent that the perfume industry generates millions of dollars per year and is fueled by advertising campaigns that cost millions in and of themselves. There are now products on the market that are designed with pheromones that help attract men or women. The degree, of course, often depends on the individual and how the blend works with body chemistry, but several people I know have had success trying them. The only downside is that unlike perfume and colognes, which you can find inexpensively, they often bear a hefty price tag for even a small amount. Then again, a little dab goes a long way!

Think about your personality for a moment. Do you consider yourself sweet? Are you hot and spicy? Is your passion a gentle heat or an all-out fire? If you had to pick some aromatics that fit your loving style, which ones would they be? Write them down in a list, and then make a sexy scent that reflects your sexual style and personality.

To start, narrow your list to three aromatics that go well together. (To start, try ginger, vanilla, and a hint of lavender.) Next, using essential oils and ¼ cup of good-quality almond oil, start your blending. Add one or two drops of essential oil at a time; mix, smell, and repeat. Trust your inner senses and your awareness of self to tell you when the blend is just right. Store this in an airtight container and dab it on your pulse points when you know you're going to need more energy in the bedroom.

Color Me Passionate

Pleasing and teasing doesn't end at the nose. What about giving your lover eye candy, too? Science has shown that colors bring out emotional reactions in people. While these reactions differ in each individual, there is no question that specific colors in your loving environment can and will affect moods and overall performance.

Let's begin by considering each color on its own terms, bearing in mind that the symbolism of color can change dramatically from culture to culture. It's certainly not all "black and white"! Speaking of that, black is a very formal color that implies social convention (think black-tie party). It also has a somewhat restful nature because we sleep at night, when it's "black" outside. For some people black can be very repressive, bringing up anxiety and fear. Use it sparingly in the loving space, especially if you, or your partner, have trouble with seasonal affective disorder (SAD) or other forms of depression.

White

White is clarity—it's clean, crisp, and precise. We think of white as symbolizing sincerity and purity. If you're trying to project a demeanor of honor, genuineness, truthfulness, and openness to your partner, this is an ideal color to wear. Alternatively, consider placing on your dining table a bundle of white flowers whose aromas also speak of your intentions, such as lily of the valley.

Red

Red's hue automatically invokes thoughts of passion, adventure, excitement, and upbeat perspectives. Studies show that having red highlights in your environment improves alertness, which is great when you want to pay attention to (and remember) those little details your lover enjoys. Use red when you need more energy and staying power. If you're concerned about projecting too much zeal too soon, balance red with white (red being more masculine, and white being feminine).

Pink

Pink tones down the intensity of red's energy. Pink is a friendlier hue. It's less "in your face" and more approachable and welcoming than red. If you're just starting to date a person, pink might be a good choice to get things off on a warm-intentioned foot. Also, if you're not looking for a long-term affair, pink is less committal than is red. An alternative is pale orange.

Orange

Next we turn to orange, the color of the harvest. Orange is very optimistic, confident, self-sufficient, joyful, and intelligent. It is not, however, considered a "hot" color by many color therapists. Use this in your loving space for good conversations (especially if you need to feel a little more sure of yourself and the subject) or to inspire happiness.

Yellow

Yellow is similar to orange in that it's aligned with the air element and therefore provides subtle conscious, communicative powers. If either you or your partner suffers from melancholy, definitely bring more yellow into your daily environment. Yellow improves the overall energy with which you're working, so if your relationship has been in a slump, that's another good reason to add touches of it to the loving space. Being the color of the sun, yellow is often associated with hope, improved fortune, and blessings.

Green

Next comes green, a very healing color that engenders understanding, honest compassion, and dependability while decreasing stress. Symbolically it represents growth and life (renewal). In relationships, use green to settle feelings of uneasiness or to improve your ability to relate to each other's situations. Alternatively, sprout-green hues help when you want your relationship to grow to new levels.

Turquoise

Between green and blue we find turquoise, a color poised for everything from attraction and charm to confidence and self-control. If you're going out on the town looking for a potential playmate, this is definitely a color to add to your wardrobe in some way. Some people find that using too much of this color emphasizes the more selfish nature, so use it as a highlight color (or carry a crystal in that color as a touchstone instead).

Blue

If you're looking for mystical or spiritual tones in your relationship, blue is a perfect choice. Bear in mind that the lightness or darkness of this color changes its personality greatly. Light blue is upbeat and optimistic, like a clear morning sky, while dark blue is more serious, but still relaxing. Other attributes that blue brings to an outfit or an environment include idealism, a touch of classic romance, truthfulness, peace, and happiness.

Purple

Purple has some characteristics of blue in that it offers deep, spiritual sensitivity and connection. It's also a color that improves leadership skills. If you want to take charge in your relationship (even if only to play alpha for one night), look to purple to stimulate that aggressive nature. Magenta is an alternative to purple that's a little more pragmatic but not as bold as red. In the loving environment, magenta inspires affection and contentment.

Brown

For creating a safe, secure, and grounded sense in your relationship, earth tones can't be beat. The color of healthy soil, deep browns are excellent for building strong foundational energy for whatever plans you have in store. Think of it as a cornerstone in your environment. The only caution with brown is that too much leads to obstinacy and inflexibility (like the rock that cannot be moved, or the wall you can't get around). If you have a strong, unwavering personality to begin with, I don't recommend using too much of this in your wardrobe or environment.

Black

Black conveys professionalism, significance, seriousness, or formality. It's probably not the best color for a date unless the event you're attending together is likewise professional, solemn, or ceremonial. Balancing that statement, this color combined with sexy fabric makes for a unique, and thinning, allure. There's nothing that says "I want serious fun" like a black negligee.

Rainbow

Any shirt, tie, scarf, or accessory that depicts rainbow hues speaks of hope, better days ahead, and overall playfulness. It's a great choice when you and your partner are heading out for an adventure or when you'd like to try something new in bed.

Astrological Ambiance

All of this is a good starting point for understanding and using colors for ambiance, but what about your partner's astrological sign? Many people who study astrology say that there are certain colors that energize and positively influence each of the twelve zodiac signs. If you'd like to try adding those colors into your environment or wardrobe, here's some basic information to get you started:

- ✦ **Aries (March 21–April 20):** Orange, red, iron, rusts, bronze tones. Bear in mind that the Aries personality is already naturally combative, competitive, outgoing, fiery, and aggressive, so keep these colors in balance with other, subtler tones.
- ✦ **Taurus (April 21–May 21):** yellow, beige, sandy tones, green, copper, silver, and gold. All of these stimulate the beauty, grace, sensitivity, and artistic sense of Taurus. It also supports the Bull's very earthy nature. Use darker tones with caution, because the Taurus personality becomes like the bull-in-a-china-shop lover when surrounded by too many earth tones.
- ✦ **Gemini (May 22–June 21):** yellow, violet, silver, and gold (also sometimes black and white for the dual nature). Rainbow hues are fun for the Gemini, who hates stagnation and adores diversity. Also try combining hues that balance one another in the hopes that your Gemini lover will stick to one decision for more than a few minutes!
- ✦ **Cancer (June 22–July 22):** green, silver, white, blue, and sea green. Take care not to wear colors that are

too drastic, because they exacerbate Cancer's emotions and nervous energies. If your loving space is very bright, try dimming the lights or using candles to keep the Cancer mate on an even keel.

+ **Leo (July 23–August 23):** Orange, yellow, gold, red, and amber tones. Of these, red is the most potent color for a Leo, but take care that it doesn't bring out the beast until you're ready! Leave it for a sexy bed dress (or even your sheets)! Gold is a good choice for those nights when you plan to lavish your Leo in luxury.

+ **Virgo (August 24–September 23):** Purple, royal blue, navy blue, green, tan, gentle silver, and gold. Typically the Virgo personality feels most at home in earth tones, so highlight them when you're feeling out of your element. Then again, changing things up once in a while will appeal to a Virgo lover's sense of whimsy and impulse. Dare to be different periodically.

+ **Libra (September 24–October 23):** pink, pale yellow, baby blue, lavender, and copper. When you want to bring out the best in yourself, wear slightly more vibrant colors, such as royal blue. When you want to bring out your Libra partner's playfulness, go for pink with a splash of an unexpected hue (like bright green). Watch the wonder in his or her eyes, and pure enjoyment. Make yourself into the gift to unwrap!

* **Scorpio (October 24–November 22):** black, deep red, crimson, steel, gold, and silver. Your best combination is black with red, but that can also be overwhelming to a lover. Be ready for anything! For Scorpio partners, make sure to change colors somewhat unpredictably, because that appeals to this sign's impulsive nature.

* **Sagittarius (November 23–December 21):** gold-red, mauve, indigo, sea blue-green, pale blue or purple, and brass and copper tones. Sagittarius values a little bit of variety, so you may find that mixing and matching best suits you or your Sagittarius partner.

* **Capricorn (December 22–January 20):** gold, silver, green, brown, black, white. The conservative tone of a Capricorn's clothing implies maturity and responsibility. People born under this sign are forever looking to make things neat and tidy. Nonetheless, don't forget to let loose periodically and go for bright and bold. In terms of a Capricorn partner, take care not to get too splashy, because this sign can develop a case of style jealousy (and start borrowing your clothes, too!).

* **Aquarius (January 21–February 19):** vibrant blue, sky blue, most metallic hues. Blue is really the best color for you to highlight your innovative, whimsical, hopeful, and intelligent nature. For the Aquarius partner, find unusual pieces of clothing

and jewelry through which to bring these colors forward. For example, if your lover has a foot fetish, wear a blue toe ring! That will appeal to the Aquarian's unconventional nature.

+ **Pisces (February 20–March 20):** nearly any pastel that stresses the oceanic colors; also silver. Pisceans have an other-worldliness about them, as if they are already "out of space and time," so combine these colors with light, wispy clothing (like chiffon) for best results. And for your Pisces partner? Instead of the chiffons, try things that are soft and welcoming to attract their empathic attention. Make yourself petable!

To amplify the way these colors affect the passionate psyche, I suggest combining them with other sensual cues (such as using astrological aromatics).

Feng Shui Fantasies

Feng shui began in the East many centuries ago as part art form and part philosophy. It's a highly intuitive approach to one's environment that adjusts both the concrete (physical) and spiritual elements of a loving space so that it's more positive and life-affirming. In brief, feng shui seeks to attract positive chi (energy) so that all energy in and around your body flows unhindered. It is a guide to living and interacting honorably, especially with nature's powers.

There are several schools of feng shui, but the one that most Westerners know is that which was brought to the United States by Professor Lin Yun. This particular method recognizes the connection between awareness and intention, just as magick does, which is why the two can work synergistically. Feng shui, matched with your own metaphysical ideology, will improve the communication among various energies in your loving space and adjust them to the level you most desire.

Each direction in your home has a specific energy. Let's begin with the north, which produces peace and a sense of centering. This might be a good place to have those difficult discussions with your mate that otherwise would get out of balance, or to work magick for an overall ambiance of peace in your home. The element associated with this direction is water, so if you're thinking of decorating, put a fish tank here and "go with the flow!" The only caution here is not to get too much water energy in this area, because it can flood out your emotions and blur the lines of clear thinking.

Northeast governs your motivation. If you're constantly putting off making serious changes in your love life, this is the spot to which you should pay attention. This region's element is earth. Too much of it (like plants, crystals, clay, or earth-toned decorations) in this region can result in a highly competitive relationship, egotism, or selfishness, while too little leads to apathy.

The east corner governs hopefulness, idealism, energy, and even a bit of wild and wonderful adventure. Wood is the keynote element, but if there's too much of it you may find yourself being very impatient with lovers or wanting them to be more outgoing than they can comfortably be in the long term. On the other hand, spending time in this area of your loving space will certainly help your ability to last the night, and will give you some fresh ideas for lovemaking!

To the southeast you have old-fashioned maturity and common sense. This is not the most exciting area, but it does improve struggling communication (both the ability to speak and to listen clearly), and it's an excellent location in which to work magick if you or your partner experience blocks to sexual creativity. The element here is wood.

The south, as you might expect, is much "hotter." This is the region for passion, attractiveness, charm, hospitality, and socialization. Typically someone starting to date again after a long time or after divorce will want to re-energize in this region. The element is fire, so perhaps meditating with a candle and focusing on your positive traits is the ideal pre-date spiritual vitamin to get things off on a good foot. The only caution in this region is that of balance—overstimulation can cause a person or relationship to burn out very quickly.

Meanwhile, the west has to do with money and the ability to enjoy those things for which you've worked. If your relationship is suffering from financial strain, pay close attention to this area. Keep it tidy and bring metallic tones such as silver and gold into that space to attract financial abundance. Also, if you're finding that your partner (or you) are becoming lazy or nonchalant about the relationship, this is a good spot to work magick to rejuvenate things (relationships take work, too!).

Northwest becomes very tidy and organized. This is what I consider the "construct" center of your home. When you want a framework, ponder it here. If you need to get your act together and really plan something, the energy here is perfect for it. Metal is the element for this part of a room or house.

Know Your Balancing Elements

The elements of any area can work together or create disparity. Water can destroy fire or it can cool it. Fire can destroy metal or refine it. Metal can destroy wood or carve it. Wood can destroy earth or grow in it. Earth can destroy water or be nourished by it. Meanwhile, water nourishes wood, wood supports fire, fire bears earth, earth supports metal, and metal holds water.

Putting this together, say your bedroom faces south. You'll typically find your relationship is stressed and that you have trouble sleeping (perhaps because of disturbing dreams). You need to improve fire's influence here to focus on play and awareness. So, add more wooden features that support that fire, be it through actual wooden items, by color, or by shapes that reflect fire.

The most important part of your loving space in this practice is the southwest. From a magickal perspective this makes sense because the south governs passion, and the west, our emotions. In feng shui, this part of any room or building rules relationships, love, luck, and understanding. Whenever your relationships seem out of whack, look to see what's in this area. If it's cluttered, clean it up. If it's clean, light a yellow candle with the intention of shining a light on any shadows, and honoring those relationships that you treasure.

While feng shui can become complicated relatively quickly, I've assembled some helps and hints for you, your bedroom, or your loving space that you can combine with the other ambiance enhancers in this chapter:

1. *Make the space warm and welcoming.* Look at your space. Does it reflect both you and your partner (and your unique pleasures)? In bedrooms specifically, find ways to transform the energy from sleep to sex and sizzle.
2. *Release any bad memories associated with your loving space.* People are normally affected by their

surroundings; however, it's time for forward thinking. Remove those things that remind you of past lovers (or worse, remind your mate of them). Get rid of old emotional baggage. This step is especially vital if you have shared this space for a long time with another lover (or lovers). You may find that moving the furniture around helps with the process.

3. *Speaking of memories—put clean sheets on the bed* (there is nothing worse than sleeping on a figurative "wet" spot), and think about adding a purgative aromatic to those linens you've used during any other recent relationship. This accomplishes two things—there's no lingering scent for your new playmate to catch (which is a huge turn-off), and on a spiritual level it releases those old, unwanted energies so you can build anew.

4. *Think of your bedroom as your relationship's altar and sacred space.* What exactly do you keep in and around this space that accents your goals for your relationship, and what hinders it? Consider moving items out of the loving space that remind you too much of mundane things (like a computer or dirty laundry). Renew the physical space, and your romance will benefit. Other things to put away include anything that cuts (increases separatist energy and thinking), that's pointy (gibes), or childish (promotes immature reactions). For

those who have small spaces, think about creating a partition out of cloth or another material that neatly hides those reminders. Find a screen or fabric that creates a good ambiance, or at least is neutral.

5. *Don't have a TV in the loving space (or if you do, leave it off).* Unless you both enjoy watching movies to get you in the mood, this actually distracts attention from your mate. This is an item best consigned to the space behind the cloth partition for the duration.

6. *If it's possible, position your bed so that you can see the doorway clearly no matter which side you lay upon.* Psychologically, this avoids feelings of vulnerability or being trapped (especially if your lover has ever been abused). Also, feng shui experts tell us that strong headboards (metal or wood) cement the foundations of a good relationship. From a more playful vantage point, it also provides you with a secure place for some of your toys.

7. *Rework your wardrobe.* Come out of your closet . . . wait, no . . . go into it! Time to clear out the old stuff that doesn't make you feel good about yourself, and start anew. Better still, this makes space for a relationship just in case this new lover turns out to be a keeper! If you have a bathroom in your loving space, that's another good spot to apply the attitude of "out with the old, in with the new."

Even if the relationship doesn't endure long-term, the lack of clutter opens the chi in your sleeping and living environment.

8. *Decorate your space to suit the mood.* We already talked about the southwest part of your loving space. This is an excellent location for some erotic art (or other pieces that reflect your personal sexual tastes, and ideally, those of your lover). Also get rid of harsh lights and go for adjustable lighting, natural lights (like broad-spectrum bulbs), fire-safe lanterns, or candles instead. Note: For those who suffer depression, the broad-spectrum bulbs should help emotional balance and improve energy levels.

9. *Do a little dance . . . make a little love:* It really does take two to tango. If you want to inspire a relationship that grows out of your passion, have items paired in twos around the room. Two candles, two boxes, two lamps . . . anything that says to your partner, "I'm ready and waiting for the right person, and I hope it's *you*."

10. *Celebrate the Sacred Self.* You are your first priority. You can't be a passionate, sexy sorceress if you're weary, tense, or out of balance in specific areas of your life. Nurture your inner relationship with your Self, inspire your best attributes, develop your talents—find those things that make you wholly *you*.

11. *Do, Re, ME ME ME:* Self-pleasure yourself. You have more right than anyone else to fondle your body.

12. *Be prepared!* Stock up on things like massage oil, finger foods, and pleasure toys, and keep them in a handy location in your loving space.

13. *Look for curvy items, such as long, soft body pillows, to have in and around your space.* These gently provide smooth, round edges over which the chi energy flows without any trouble whatsoever.

The results from feng shui are not meant to be dramatic, but rather subtle, paced, and long-lasting. You probably will notice distinct shifts in your home's energy when you use this methodology. It's not like a sudden explosion of vibrations; it's more like a gentle wave or tantalizing breeze being let loose that adjusts the aura of not only the space, but also the people abiding therein. Perhaps that's why feng shui means "wind and water." In any case, you may have to experiment a bit to see which of these suggestions helps the most, depending on the area with which you have to work. To help yourself, keep a small notebook in which you can write down before-and-after observations over several days. This will come in handy when you plan future passionate encounters.

music is the mediator between the spiritual and the sensual life.

ludwig van beethoven

Flirting

all in a sensual day, all in a playful way

It's easy to forget that passion isn't like a water faucet that can be turned on and turned off at a whim. However, by learning how to make flirting into a magickal talent, you can slowly build passionate energy throughout the day. That way, by the time you and your mate are ready for a date, your body and spirit will be ready as well!

Many people do not realize that flirting is a very important part of interacting with people. Every culture and society around the world has its own customs of flirting; in times past it was even celebrated as an art form. In fact, there are even individuals in today's world (particularly in larger metropolitan areas) who make their living as flirting coaches. We've so lost touch with this important means of interpersonal communication that it's now been relegated to a job description!

Biologically speaking, flirting is part of our nature. During the times when we lived much shorter life spans, this aptitude helped humankind find potential sex partners for reproduction. While the world has become very different since those days, that doesn't mean that the instinct to flirt has disappeared. People simply express it in new ways to reflect current lifestyle(s) and human progress. If you feel clueless about how to flirt, or just plain insecure, read on!

You may be wondering, what's so magickal about understanding flirting? Flirting is driven by biology, emotions, and social etiquette, but magick? Why? That's a good question, and one that deserves some attention. Your body, mind, and spirit are all interconnected. The more you understand of your mind and body, the more able you will be to direct your spiritual energy toward a goal. The rule of *know thyself* applies on all levels of BE-ing. Once you begin to understand how you think, you will be better able to understand your behavior, because thought drives action. The more you understand your behavior, the more easily you can predict how various thoughtful actions promote reactions in those toward whom you're directing your attention.

There are subtle and overt forms of flirting. Some people do not pick up on subtle cues, especially body language. So as you're educating yourself about these things, you may want to share your insights with potential lovers and friends who might also need some help in interpreting various "come ons" and how serious they may (or may not) be. This alleviates a lot of guesswork for everyone involved, and also puts people more at ease.

Like all other human interactions, flirting has some general do's and don'ts. The rest of this chapter shares some guidelines that you can apply readily and easily to your sexy sorcery. Let's begin with the where, who, and how of this art.

Flirting Spaces

Some places are obviously inappropriate for flirting because of the nature of what happens therein. For example, you wouldn't want to flirt at a funeral home. That's truly poor taste! However, other social occasions offer just the opposite—a setting in which flirting is actually expected and typically very acceptable. A party is a time to have fun, explore, and meet-and-greet to your heart's content. If you meet someone with potential, you can unleash your unbridled sensual sorceress charm.

Though parties are a great playground for flirting, you need to use caution here if you're imbibing.

Alcohol dulls the senses, particularly your intuition and common sense. Your judgment may be off, which can lead to very awkward moments and apologies. To help with this, carry or wear a charged, blessed amethyst the next time you plan to drink and flirt. The Romans believed that amethysts could be used to cure drunkenness. While that may be a bit of a stretch, the amethyst crystal does have strong balancing energies, and its entire matrix helps with self-control and centering. If you feel your discretion slipping, hold the amethyst between your palms, and breathe deeply and evenly until you know you're back on track. Then have a glass or two of water.

It's also a good idea to carry this stone if you're going out dancing, to an eatery, or to any type of drinking establishment. Even if you're not drinking yourself, the stone will protect you from all of the discordant energy flying around and thus help you focus your flirting more effectively.

While meeting a partner at a bar has gotten somewhat of a bad rap in our society and has even become a bit of a joke, statistics indicate that 25 percent of current couples say that's exactly how they met their mate! If you're using this type of public setting to woo and seduce, it's important to provide the intended person with a safe space in which to approach you. To help with this, you can consider creating a semiformal sacred space. Witches of old used to cast spells by drawing a circle around a space they wanted to keep safe. The circle set up a boundary of energy that kept out what they didn't want and allowed entrance of what they wanted to experience. How can you adapt this idea?

Well, try visualizing a pink-white bubble of light that surrounds you on all sides—but leave an opening in the direction of the person in whom you have interest (pink expresses friendly feelings, while white protects). You can mentally close that doorway if the wrong person approaches, and you can also close the door once the intended person enters the space so you won't get interrupted by the noise and crowds!

Body language is another important part of magick and flirting. It expresses those things that you might not be wholly ready to say out loud, and also provides a signal of intention that the Universe can easily interpret. Accidentally brush up against your crush on the way to your seat. Offer a humble apology, make brief eye contact, and then sit down. From there, look up again and wait for that person to look toward you. As soon as he or she does, lower your eyes. As this look-toward-look-away ritual progresses, slowly increase the amount of time your eyes lock, and add other little touches like fondling a straw, adjusting a piece of clothing, uncrossing your arms or legs (a signal of openness), or gently playing with a strand of hair.

Another good location for flirting is an educational setting (such as activities at a college, a special class in a field of personal talent, or a lecture). The beauty of this locale is that you're around people with similar interests and a common goal, thus making it much easier to find a topic of conversation. Try these helpful hints:

+ Smile when an interesting person goes by. As you do, mentally add a little charm to the process, such as, "see my smile, come sit for a while!"
+ Put any clunky items in a chair or another safe location and watch your bearing. Think of having a pole of silver that supports your spine (silver is intuitive, and the visualization actually helps improve posture). This relays confidence without being overly pushy.
+ Wear clothing that moves with you (this is even more effective if you've charged the clothing with aromatic oils or herbs in the dryer beforehand). Note that if you want to work with the aromatherapy angle, light and airy clothing helps diffuse the scent to the surroundings.
+ Make eye contact periodically. Remember that the eyes are the windows of your soul. Let your sensual sorceress out!

You can also put some specially prepared powder in your shoes to get your romance off on the right foot.

Take cornstarch and add some finely ground rosemary to it. Sprinkle it in the bottoms of your shoes or use it to lightly dust your feet. Rosemary has a clean fragrance that is reputed to enhance memory and powers of concentration. Good for exam time, and if you do catch the name of a sexy classmate, you'll remember it! Better yet, suggest a study date and bring along a snack or dinner infused with rosemary. You can also add aromatics (see Chapter 2) that mirror your goals.

Another potential venue for flirting is work. Like the educational setting, you are apt to find people here

---

activity • insightful sunglasses

A pair of sunglasses is a great prop for your sexy sorcery kit. Sunglasses allow you to peruse a room without anyone being the wiser. Before you go out, however, bless and charge them with good energy so that you can "see" clearly, and find the best possible mate. To do so, dab the rims of the glasses with just a little sandalwood, jasmine, or lavender oil, all of which improve psychic awareness. Lightly run your finger clockwise around the rim of the glasses while repeating:

Inner vision come to me
Only the truth let me see
These glasses when placed upon my eyes
Reveal all, and banish lies.

Slip on your sexy shades and get ready to flirt!

---

with similar backgrounds and interests. Mind you, this is a space where flirting has to be approached very carefully. Every employer has ground rules about what is considered appropriate. Discretion is key in this space—one wrong move and you could end up with a lawsuit or a pink slip. (Talk about heavy magick!)

That being said, many people do meet their spouses and partners in their jobs. In any case, take care to maintain a professional demeanor and stick with the etiquette of the work zone. To help with this, keep a carnelian at your desk as a touchstone. Carnelian helps ensure that your communications are clearly understood, no matter the conversation's purpose. Also consider dabbing the area around your personal workspace with a meaningful aromatic. This is kind of like marking your territory, but more important, you can choose the aromatic so it matches your goals of keeping away some people, and attracting others.

Decisions, Decisions

The next step in the flirting game is figuring out whether you're flirting seriously or just having some fun. There are times when you want to engage in playful banter without worrying that you'll be taken the wrong way or possibly hurt someone. In fact, studies indicate that playful flirtation can be very healthy for

To keep your flirting light, try this activity. On the night of a full moon (the full moon supports your intuitive sense so you don't go too far), take a feather out beneath the moonlight. Cup it in your hands and repeat:

Tickle my fancy with flirtatious play
Let none misunderstand what I do or say
Beneath the stars and full-moon's light
Let my spell take to flight.

Carry the feather with you and release it to a desktop or other surface just before you intend to banter.

self-esteem and even improve the overall environment in which it takes place. Let's face it, whether you're single, married, or committed in another way, it feels really good to have that periodic admiring glance or compliment.

However, be careful that your playful flirting isn't read or interpreted the wrong way. Make sure the object of your affection is clear about your intentions. Jealousy nullifies the benefits of playful flirting pretty quickly. What's more, seducing someone who has more of an emotional investment in the game sets up an energy pattern that may feed your ego but not your karma. Practice magick with respect! How? Be clear about your intentions—whatever they are.

Intentioned flirting is different from playful flirting in that you're actively looking for a mate, or for a date that has mating potential. There have been some interesting findings on this subject if that's the route you've decided to take. For example, as superficial as it sounds, people who possess the same level of physical attractiveness tend to have stronger and longer relationships. The challenge, of course, is in gauging attractiveness, which is a subjective quality. Moreover, most people tend to dramatically over- or underestimate their level of attractiveness. Again, it comes back to being honest with yourself, and your potential partner, and then flirt on that level with your intentions in mind. Also, remember that beauty is in the eye of

aromatic attractiveness

If you're looking to accent the positive, dab your power centers (chakras) with vetivert. This herb has the wonderful ability to change the way it smells according to your unique body chemistry and aura, meaning it can project whatever image and message you most want to potential partners. As you apply it, visualize in detail how you want to be seen, as well as your overall goals for that social situation. If you can take a small vial of refresher oil with you, all the better. Use it when you sense yourself losing confidence.

the beholder. A certain look, inflection of the voice, or quality of personality can be beautiful. Think sexy and you will be sexy!

Flirting 101

Once you know what your flirting goal is, the question remains as to how to flirt effectively. Some people seem to have a natural flirting ability, but for most of us it's often an embarrassing or frustrating trial-and-error proposition. However, with a little magick and intuition, you can lessen the "error" portion as much as possible.

Flirting consists of both verbal and nonverbal cues. Most people, particularly men, are far more aware of the verbal element. They look for word cues but don't always grasp subtler meanings beneath the conversation (men typically think in a very logical, progressive manner—A + B = C—not intuitively). Unfortunately, it's the other cues that really make or break your flirtations.

At least 50 percent of the impression you make has nothing to do with what you say at all! Your posture, the way you move, and your facial expression speak volumes to potential lovers before you ever say a word. On the upside of the equation, nonverbal flirting is easier emotionally. The risk of embarrassment and rejection are minimized dramatically in comparison to verbal flirting.

By far, your eyes are the biggest flirting tool you possess. Dorothy Parker once wrote "Men don't make passes at girls who wear glasses." As someone who cannot wear contacts, believe me—glasses create an unnecessary barrier to the message you hope to convey. Don't despair! How you remove your glasses, however, can speak volumes and be a sexy act in and of itself (kind of like letting your hair down)! From that point forward, the way you look at a person, how long you maintain eye contact, and when you look away from him or her can make or break the moment. You don't have to see the person clearly as long as you know toward whom your intention is directed.

Start with short glances. Men interpret longer periods of eye contact (especially with other men) as a challenge or an implication of hostile intention. Women, by comparison, often interpret this behavior as a message of trust, confidence, or love. So gauge your gaze carefully and think about the meaning behind it (in magick, meaning is everything).

If the other person doesn't respond with some type of nod or smile, or doesn't maintain eye contact for more than a second or two on the second try, you're probably out of luck. Knowingly or not, our bodies betray our desires. Mind you, the person could be with a friend and therefore uncomfortable about flirting, or could be shy. The best action is to observe the person discreetly for a while to see if you can pick up on more specific signals that will help you decide whether or not to approach him or her.

Let's say this goes well and you want to take the next step and start up a conversation with this person. As you approach, make eye contact once more. As you talk, periodically glance at the person's face, especially when he or she is speaking. Continue to keep eye contact brief so you don't convey too much intimacy too soon or mislead the person. However, looking at the wrong place while talking is also a turnoff. No one likes to feel that a conversation is a cheap excuse to get a better view of their cleavage or butt!

While talking, pay particular attention to whether the person stays in place, gets closer, or moves back. This will help you find a comfortable body space, which in turn will help that person relax and not feel threatened or pushed. The standard comfort zone for a good conversation is usually about 4 feet (note that if you're in a noisy or overcrowded bar it gets hard to talk, so you may wish to suggest moving to a place where you can speak without being too forward with personal space).

If the conversation goes well you can try to move in, but never closer than about 18 inches, which is what most humans reserve for intimacy. While studies show that what people consider "too close for comfort" is often culturally dictated, this is a good basic rule of thumb that usually keeps you clear of any misunderstandings. You can also use a carnelian as a charm in your pocket to improve your verbal acumen—it's a strong communication stone. Alternatively, wear something yellow to honor the air element, which helps to motivate positive discourse.

The second element of nonverbal communication is bearing, or stance. If your posture belies boredom, it doesn't matter how interested your eyes or smile appear; people are going to think you don't care. Watch your stance and that of the person with whom you're flirting. Slouching, feet turning slightly away, or arms folded across the body are three signs on either person's part that attention is waning, that you've hit a sensitive subject, or that there's an unspoken disagreement with a statement. On the other hand, a tilt of the head and an open stance, such as the person turning his or her full body toward you, is a much more inviting sign. When the person begins mirroring your stance, that's even better because it symbolizes rapport, agreement, and harmony.

Gestures, which are the third nonverbal clue, come hand-in-hand with bearing. Movement is like the patterns of magick. It can accentuate or completely destroy conversation, and it provides another level of footnotes to the nonverbal cues already discussed. While gestures also can have strong cultural influences, the rule of thumb throughout human society is that the more lively the gesture, the greater level of interest and attention. Some gestures, such as rubbing one's palms or scratching, signal negative interest/attention and anxiety. Other gestures, such as nodding, reveal active listening and focus on the part of a listener. If you want to use nodding, pace it to match the speaker, giving a nod once in a while. Just as with stance, people who like each other naturally begin to mirror each other. If you're really in sync with your partner mirroring responses will probably just happen when that special moment occurs and everything just fits together. A fourth thing to pay attention to is the tapestry of facial expressions. From a gentle smile to raised eyebrow, expressions create an entire language. The key difficulty is learning what the person really intends to convey, versus what he or she does for social convention. How often have you had to control laughter or tears to suit the circumstance? Most people have been trained since a very young age to stay in control,

activity • expression interpretation

If you're not certain what a person's expression conveys, then it's a good time to put some of your spiritual instincts to good use. If, for example, you're good at sensing auras, check out the target person. Rough, dark, tight auras often indicate a closed personality. By comparison, bright, big, smooth auras are far more welcoming. One quick tip for noticing a person's energy field is to look at how others respond to him or her. Do they move closer or pull away? Do people's moods change as they interact with that person? This is a fun exercise if you're observing someone from across a room. If you're not good at auric reading, don't despair. Simply take a nice deep breath as you observe, and pay attention to that small voice within, which will rarely lead you astray. Listen to what comes up, and act accordingly.

so it becomes very hard to know when you're getting a sincere expression rather than an all-plastic, go-for-image, no-substance glance.

Generally speaking, unexpressive faces equal a lack of interest, a sense that the topic of conversation is unsettling, or that the individual is trying to remain as an observer. Amusement, agreement, inquiries, and introductions all gain much more attention when accompanied with a comfortable-looking expression. Smiling when you hear something that makes you more at ease or happy is a good example. Without the smile, much could be lost in translation, as it often is in e-mail.

The fifth nonverbal cue is perhaps the most difficult to master for many people—that of touch. We know from psychological studies that touch is important to human wellness and social interaction. Unfortunately for us, the exact same touch (depending on the person or situation) can convey a message of worry, interest, directing attention, approval, acceptance, questioning, greeting, or affection (just to name a few). It's easy to send mixed signals no matter how well-intentioned you may be. So if someone gets the wrong message, try to clarify so no hurt feelings ensue.

Be aware that the level of touch that's acceptable in any setting not only depends on the culture of the individual and society, but also on personality and personal space issues. Almost universally, however, a brief touch to the arm, shoulder, or hand conveys some level of interest, the hand being the most intimate outside of a handshake-style greeting. A pat on the back is also pretty acceptable as a show of support, while not being overtly sensual or sexual. In any case, you'll know pretty quickly if you've stepped over any intimacy lines with someone. The person will move back, frown, suddenly stop talking, or turn away.

Because touching can lead to far more sensual moments, one should proceed slowly with this type of communication, especially in public. As with eye contact, touch briefly and see how the person responds. Wait for the person to return a look or touch to confirm the "go-ahead." This probably sounds terribly mundane, but many people are never taught about the language of touch, eye contact, and other nonverbal cues, so it's no wonder we misunderstand each other! We will talk more deeply about truly sensual and magickal touching in Chapter 4.

Talking the Talk

Flirting has many dimensions. Now it's time to consider the verbal cues. The first thing you need to realize about speech is that what you say, how you say it, and all your other nonverbal cues matter. For example, say someone rushes a greeting or speaks without inflection while barely making eye contact. You can pretty well assume that he or she is distracted, shy, incredibly nervous, or uninterested. Similarly, being too quiet implies fear, depression, or a less aggressive personality. Moderate tones with regular variances are the best way to keep nearly any person's attention, because these are the "middle of the road" no matter the personality type.

activity • do you hear what i hear?

Most people have no idea how other people hear their voices. This activity will help you become more aware of that and teach you how to adjust your tone to reflect your intention. To begin, you'll need a portable tape recorder and tapes. Record any conversation you're having with someone close. Play it back. Notice in particular the tones or voice variances that say "I care" and those that imply your closeness.

Next, write down some of the phrases that are likely to come up in a discussion with someone new—your interests, your job, and so on. Say these phrases into your recorder using several different tones—one excited, one slow and steady, one lacking real inflection, and so on. Now listen again. Write down what you notice about the subtle signals your voice is sending with each change in tone. Use this knowledge and awareness when you engage in your next verbal flirting session.

Loud or Low?

Dropping your volume in a discussion is often interpreted as either a come-hither action or an invitation to speak (most often the latter). The rest of the nonverbal cues we've discussed thus far should help fill in the rest of the dating (single mingle) equation. For many people, flirting is a natural aptitude. The real problem lies in just starting a conversation, not finishing it! However, some people don't realize that their companion's voice may drop off momentarily to gather a thought, or reconsider the way he or she is communicating an idea. Then, if you begin talking, that person thinks you rude! This is not uncommon in male-female interactions. The key is finding a good middle ground in your conversation and tone and learning about the people in whom you have a sincere interest.

Which brings us to the subject of infamous pickup lines. Men and women alike laugh about these, but truth be told, creative conversation making can (and often does) make or break a potential flirtation. Nonetheless, it can't hurt to carry a little magickal help in your pocket. You can use any yellow stone as a charm (yellow is associated with the air element, which also deals with our conscious mind) for effective speech.

Once the conversation is rolling along, how well things progress depends on your listening skills as well as overall social ease and the setting. Hearing is also tied to the air element. If you find that you easily lose

breath mint communication charm

Breath mints are one of my favorite components for positive communication. The symbolic value is perfect—having your words drip off a sweet tongue. Just gather up your container of mints before you go out into a social situation and empower them with an incantation like this one:

Tongue be nimble, tongue be quick,
Secure my magick in these mints!

You can repeat the incantation just before consuming one.

your focus in conversations, you may want to buy an empowering oil to take with you. Try lily of the valley, as it is an air-oriented aromatic, and will improve your overall mental awareness throughout a conversation no matter how tempted you might be to drift off into fantasies.

As your companion opens up a little more, match that trust by opening up yourself. This doesn't mean that you have to "tell all," but if the person shares a personal like or dislike, counter with one of your own. This maintains a balance in the conversation, so that neither person feels overexposed. This allows your auras to match, which in turn makes for better intimacy later, if you so choose.

Another excellent tool in conversation is humor. It helps to alleviate stress and brings two people into the same frame of mind. If, for example, the discussion has been going very well and you're hoping to increase the possibilities for more intimacy, a slightly sexy joke can help make that transition smoother. Also, if your hope is that this encounter might be more than a one-night stand, humor is very important. It's among the keynotes that make for lasting relationships. Just don't go overboard. Listen carefully so you know when your partner is being serious and when he or she is trying to lighten the mood; otherwise, the resulting misunderstandings could be disastrous.

If you are looking for a charm to infuse your humor, try a feather. Bless it by saying:

> *Tickle my fancy, tickle me pink*
> *Magick's the chain, filled with joy—link by link*
> *Let humor fill my wit and my mind*
> *In this feather, this magick I bind.*

Gently drop the feather in the vicinity of the conversation.

When at last it's time to go, the conversation has wound down, and a critical moment occurs, you need to ask yourself if there is a true mutual attraction. If so (in salesmen's terms) you need to close the deal by offering another meeting or a phone number. Don't be afraid to get specific here. If you want to get together, it's okay to go so far as to present a potential time and place for doing so, especially if the activity ties into something you've already discussed (such as a mutual hobby).

By the way, it's a great idea to have premade cards with your number and e-mail address on them. For one thing, you know that it's legible! You can also add a little magick by blessing them and/or dabbing them with magickal oil (or your perfume) before you head out.

Rallying from Rejection

Even when you're using magick as a helpmate, it's not your place to constrain another person's free will. Even with sexy sorcery at your disposal, you are going to periodically experience rejection. Don't let this become a huge downer. It happens to everyone, and without risk there's also no reward. More than likely, you're much better off. The object of your affection is not doing you any favors by leading you on when no real interest exists. Moreover, trying to hold on to what doesn't belong to you just sends a message to the Universe that you're desperate—and the Universe always brings you more of what you send out. Instead, use the rejection to turn your attention toward more suitable personalities. Don't let it cloud your judgment or create paranoia, because that will negatively affect future flirting adventures.

Being prepared emotionally, physically, and spiritually helps a lot. Meditate before you go into social situations. Find your center and really get grounded in who and what you are as a whole person. It is that person you want to present to people.

You can boost your self-confidence after a recent rejection by wearing or carrying something unusual

activity • confidence meditation

Begin by sitting comfortably (already dressed in your chosen clothing for the outing). Close your eyes and breathe deeply. If you notice that any muscle is tense, mindfully relax it. Continue to breathe slowly and evenly in through your nose and out through your mouth so that one breath naturally connects with the next. Begin to imagine a sparkling gold light pouring down into your body from above. Gold is the color of leadership, courage, and self-awareness. Continue to visualize that gold energy filling you until you feel as if you can hold no more. If you wish, this is a particularly good time to use affirmations, too. Repeat "I am confident" or "I am sexy" throughout the meditation to reinforce the visualization. When you're done, slowly return your breathing to normal and then take all that golden power with you into the social situation.

that will help open conversations for you. Perhaps you have a cool scarf, an antique money clip, or an unusual piece of jewelry. Such items often alleviate nervousness because the focus is less personal. You can discuss the object instead of something more intimate.

Second, don't just jump into the flirting game when you're feeling a little off, or if you think you're honestly not ready yet. It's okay to take time to regroup and recoup. When you feel ready, it's also wise to get a feel for the dynamics of the social situation that you are considering.

Finally, don't get hung up on being perfect. You are a wholly unique magickal being who has a great deal to offer to others. You don't need to be the "ideal" beauty or buff guy to be attractive. Just be yourself and celebrate that person. It's really true that the more you love and appreciate yourself, the easier it becomes for other people to be attracted to you.

to me luxury is to be at home with
my daughter, and the occasional
massage doesn't hurt!

olivia newton-john

Magickal Massage

and other amorous adventures

he skin is the largest sensory organ of the human body. Maybe that explains why we have a natural need for touch. In fact, it's necessary for healthy human development. Studies have shown that babies who are held and caressed develop cognitive skills more quickly and have stronger immune systems than do babies who are neglected. The other sense that's very important to sensuality is the sense of smell. Your sense of smell is very important in manifesting desire. Think about how your mouth waters when you catch a whiff of your favorite food. The scent each person has is unique—and it speaks volumes to those with whom we're intimate. Combine these two senses with a bit of magick and you've got a winning way of telling your lover when to go slow, and when to come here now!

Aroma and touch are an effective way of initiating intimate communications between individuals. Moreover, touch can be used to soothe, comfort, and heal the body. Massage is a great example of how touch, particularly when combined with aroma, can be used to heal. Massage naturally increases circulation, which in turn balances and stimulates the sexual arousal hormones. Before you begin, however, let's take a short look at where the ideas behind sensual massage originate and how you can adapt them to your practices.

History of Massage

The art of massage is one of the oldest forms of body care. Egyptian tombs have illustrations of massage, while books from China dating to 2,700 B.C.E. recommend massage as a treatment for illness. In both Greece and Rome it was one of the methods most utilized by physicians, including Hippocrates, who wrote, "but assuredly in rubbing . . . for rubbing can bind a joint that is too loose, and loosen a joint that is too rigid." It seems our ancestors had the right idea, especially considering that massage is used today in many medical and physical therapy settings. It's also often part of holistic therapies such as reflexology, aromatherapy, and osteopathy.

Massage in Brief Review

3000 B.C.E.—CHINA

Oldest known book about massage is written

2500 B.C.E.—EGYPT

Reflexology is born

1800 B.C.E.—INDIA

Ayurvedic writings focus on sensual massage

1000 B.C.E.—GREECE

Poet Homer wrote about oils used for massage

460–380 B.C.E.—GREECE

Hippocrates used rubbing to treat sprains

100–44 B.C.E.—ROME

Julius Caesar used massage therapy to relieve epilepsy (he used it most of his life due to his condition)

100 C.E.—CHINA

First schools of massage developed

600 C.E.—JAPAN

Development of shiatsu

1517–1590—FRANCE

Ambroise Pare, a French surgeon, advocated massage

1660–1742—PRUSSIA

The royal physician recommended rubbing gymnasts performing for the court

1828–1917—UNITED STATES

American osteopathic medicine begins

1894—UNITED KINGDOM

Society of Trained Masseuses formed in Britain

1927—UNITED STATES

Formation of the New York State Society of Medical Massage Therapists

1991—UNITED STATES

Touch Research Institute created

In addition, the concept of using massage for sexual arousal and gratification has been in practice for as long as massage has existed. In tantric massage, the intent is to weave sacred sexual energies together to inspire wholeness. Though less lofty, Cleopatra's lover, Mark Antony, massaged her feet to please and tease her. And, of course, one can't overlook the Kamasutra—the ultimate love manual—that encourages couples to try all manner of erotic methods, including massage, for pleasure.

Auric Massage

Touch is a powerful means of communication; thus, before you give or receive a massage, it's important to examine the spiritual aspect of what you're doing. Each person's body has an energy field surrounding it, an atmospheric envelope of sorts, called an aura. This subtle field of energy conveys messages about everything that's going on within the individual. This means that any stress or sickness your lover is holding will be expressed through that energy field. Additionally, the entire pattern of a person's character is contained in the aura. You can't get much more intimate than that!

It's vital to acquaint yourself with your partner's energy. For one thing, as you become more aware of it, you'll be able to satisfy his or her unspoken needs and desires more readily. Additionally, you'll be able to cue in more quickly when something isn't quite right—then lend a hand to fix it! Such sensitivity will lead to much more interesting and fulfilling sexual encounters.

The easiest way to begin is for you and your partner to sit in comfortable chairs across from each other. Hold out your hands palm down, and have your partner's hands beneath yours, palms up. Begin where you're nearly touching and wait until you feel heat in the space between your hands. Both of you should breathe deeply and evenly in unison. Don't force this process; just let yourselves get in sync. Now begin to move your hands further apart by about three-quarters of an inch at a time. Do you still feel that energy dancing between your palms and your partner's? Excellent! Though this is a very simple activity, it will make both of you much more aware of each other's energies and how to align yourselves with one another energetically.

Next, take what you've observed during the previous exercise and exchange auric massages with your partner. To begin, have your partner lie down. Again, your partner can remain fully clothed for this (though undressing might add to the sensual appeal). Before you start, breathe in unison, and shake any nervousness or anxiety out of your hands. If you or your partner are holding on to stress or fear it can accidentally be transferred into the aura, creating the opposite effect of what you want!

auric signals

Some people get messages when they're working with another person's auric envelope. You may feel something with your hands; smell, hear, or taste something; or even see colors. If any of this happens, make a mental note of it and share the information with your partner. It can prove very helpful in understanding him or her and offers insights into issues of which he or she may be unaware. For example, seeing hot red in an aura can indicate repressed anger that needs to be released. Smelling a light floral aroma indicates overall happiness and well-being. While many books have been written about what each signal means, what's most important is what those signals immediately mean to *you*.

Begin at your partner's head. Put your hands, again palm down, about 12 inches away from his or her body. Wait until you start to sense the auric envelope. It could feel like heat, tingling, or pressure. If you don't sense anything, move in a little closer until you connect.

Move your hands gently, slowly, and evenly down from head to foot as if to smooth out a blanket. Do this three times in each location, continuing to move from head to toe until you've smoothed the entire exterior of the aura. As you do, remember two things. First, remain very aware of anything that you feel in the aura that doesn't seem to belong. A good way to determine this is to listen to the sensual cues you receive. If you are working on one part of your partner's aura and you see the color black or receive an unpleasant sensation, that usually means the aura is holding some negative energy. Spend extra time smoothing out those spots so your partner is totally balanced when you're finished.

Second, visualize a sparkling white light pouring into your partner from the palms of your hands as you go. White has a healing and cleansing vibration and will release tension. Once you know your partner is relaxed, you can change the color you're visualizing to something like pink or a warmer hue to heat things up to the next level.

Have your partner repeat the process for you. You may find that what you experience during this is surprisingly dramatic! The near-touching of the process teases the senses in ways that hard touch does not. Because this practice can be quite powerful, make a mental note of what worked best for both of you so you can use it again.

Rub Them the Right Way

Massage is basically a patterned stroking, rubbing, or kneading of the skin and soft tissues to induce relaxation. Once a person is relaxed, he or she is also much more open to intimacy on every level of being. The first step, however, is to ensure you'll have enough time and privacy for this (don't forget to turn off the phone!). You'll want to savor the process, be it giving or receiving, without distraction.

Second, prepare yourself and your space. Consider starting out with a wonderful, long bath. Again, you can use the power of fragrance to deepen the sensory response. Add passionate aromatics to the water or hang a bunch of spicy herbs in the shower to set the tone. As you're bathing, focus on opening your senses fully. Inhale deeply. Feel the warmth of the water slipping over your skin. Go ahead and indulge in a little playful fantasy so that your senses start to hum.

Once you've toweled off, set up incense and candles, play soft music around the massage area—add anything that enhances the mood. Turn up the heat a bit so neither one of you gets cold (or use the air conditioning if it's a particularly sticky day). You'll probably want to do this on a bed or couch for comfort. Speaking of which, don't forget to dress comfortably, too! Loose clothing that's easily removable is the best choice. Towels and robes work perfectly.

Let your partner decide whether to start the massage face up or face down. Offer a blindfold to block out any unwanted light and to raise the level of suspense. Place a rolled, warm (or cold) towel or soft pillow under your partner's ankles (face down) or knees (face up) for greater comfort.

hint

Before the massage. dab aromatics on whatever you are wearing so that the garment puts you in the best frame of mind. I like to toss my robe into the dryer with a bundle of ginger, lavender, and rose (for energy, peace, and love). The heat of the dryer releases the scent and the energies of those aromatics into the clothing.

Next, make sure to have some lubricant. You can use oil-based or water-based oils, but take care. Avoid getting too close to genitals with oil because it can cause infections, and avoid anything to which your partner has had an allergic reaction in the past (if time allows, pretest the oil on a small patch of skin just to be on the safe side). Also, some oils can eat through condoms—important to keep in mind if you're hoping your sensual massage will lead to other things. You can also consider making your own aromatic oil blend using a base of sunflower or almond oil with scents added into it that express your desire (refer to Chapter 2 for specific ideas about magickal scents).

Don't Be Shy

Once you've set the space and the mood, and both of you are ready to begin, communication becomes an important part of erotic massage. Both of you have to feel comfortable and aware of each other, and comfortable expressing your pleasure. Talk about whether you enjoy a light or hard touch. Ask when you need a break, and mention when the temperature in the room is uncomfortable for you. These subjects are "light" talk that can also open up the conversation to more intimate matters. The first time you give or receive an erotic massage can prove awkward—even for longtime lovers, let alone a new person. Also be aware that sensual massage does *not* always have to lead to sex. Discuss your goals together and stay within any guidelines that build trust.

Having said that, sensual sorcery includes intimate playtime. So as you feel so inclined, express what you like. Tell your partner that he or she is sexy! Put as much magick and creativity into your words as possible, whispering of your desires on all levels. If you wish, you can even make up a chant that either one of you can recite (or say it together, slowly at first, letting the volume and speed naturally rise with your excitement levels). Here's an example:

Raise higher, higher
Passion's fire!
Magick takes flight
As our bodies ignite!

Alternatively, you could walk your partner through a visualization that will let him or her indulge in a mental fantasy that you know will be heightened by the massage. This is very similar to guided meditation, except your goals are a little more pleasurable. Use the energy of your voice and let yourself visualize as you speak for the best, most energized results.

Here's an example based on a fantasy called "the stranger":

"See yourself walking down a dusty country road. The moon is shining brightly overhead. All around you the sounds of night sing as if serenading the silvery light. The wind is warm and gentle, carrying your shirt softly in all directions and caressing your skin." (Pause to let the imagery settle in.)

"Ahead on the road there's a fork. Trees surround it, making a natural archway. Within stands a _____ (man or woman depending on your partner's preference) whose face is framed by leaves. S/he almost seems to be part of the land—quiet and still, sure and welcoming. S/he sees you and smiles a knowing little smile. This is the person you've dreamed about. S/he is waiting for you." (Pause again for anticipation).

From this point you can vary the visualization according to your partner's preferences and fantasies. Use images and scenarios that you know tantalize him or her. Let yourself fantasize too!

Relaxing the Body

Remember the earlier exercise of breathing in unison that you and your partner used during the auric work? This is a good time to connect that way again. Make eye contact (if your partner is face up and not wearing a blindfold). Place your oil set within easy reach and stand or sit comfortably nearby.

Put your hands to rest in a central location on your partner's body. Stay still and breathe. Feel the rhythm of the person beneath your hands. When he or she starts to relax, the breathing will even out.

Now gently glide your hands over the skin, but not so light that it tickles. Get into a pattern and flow so that one movement harmonizes with the next. Don't do anything too intimate at this point; just caress your partner.

You can begin to rub a little more firmly after the first pass, but again, be careful. Some people are very sensitive, and this massage is for pleasure. Work on the arms, legs, hands, feet. Don't overlook anything that seems tense. Then, do the other side, taking care to use more lubrication when you feel your hands getting too dry to glide smoothly.

By the time you're done with the second pass on both sides, most people are usually ready for something more. Take a moment and spot-check your partner. Make sure that there's some kind of body or eye signal that says it's okay to progress. Again, this builds trust, which in turn improves intimacy. When you've got the go-ahead, gently massage erotic regions. From here on out your job is to sweep up and down the body so that every sensation ties into the erotic zones. Slowly but surely you're building arousal levels. Let nature, your understanding of your partner, and your inner sensual sorcerers take over from here!

Massage for Healing and Comfort

Not everything about sensual sorcery need be focused on sexuality. In fact, if your partner is feeling off, sad, or discouraged, it's going to be very difficult to get anything started! Additionally, showing your partner that you're putting his or her needs first, and being really attentive to subtle cues, makes for much more intimate and intense sensual encounters at another time. Thoughtfulness acts as a very powerful inspiration.

We know from research that gentle massage and touching improves the release of the body's feel-good chemicals (endorphins). That's really no surprise, because the skin has 5 million sensory receptors. Massage also stimulates a person's natural healing abilities and aids in relaxation. Since both of these sound perfect for your goal of relaxing and refreshing your partner, the next obvious question is how to best go about the process.

It's important to approach the healing massage differently—in modality and, most important, in your spiritual intention. Begin by washing your hands. As you do, visualize rinsing away any self-centered energy so that you can entirely focus on your partner. Also, because we associate hand washing with sanitary practices, you can also focus on your personal aura so you can clean away any negativity there too. Envision the bubbles from the soap rising up your hands and dancing around your body, collecting everything you don't want or need and then neatly rinsing it all down the drain!

Before your partner arrives, you may want to consider the overall atmosphere in your space. Make sure the room is comfortably warm. If you have a heating pad, you can use that on the massage surface under a sheet. You also may want to warm up towels in the dryer (complete with some soothing herbs, such as lavender). Put on some soothing music, and lay out a small sampling of your partner's favorite comfort foods.

Include some magickal beverages or munchies that will replace the blues with happiness and wholeness. Here are a few recipes for you to try.

Excellent Eggnog (Serves 2)

Eggs have wonderful mystical connotations. People used them as talismans to banish illness, just as you want to banish negative energies. Additionally, Finnish mythology says that the cosmos hatched from a huge egg, which provides the extra symbolism of new beginnings and renewal. The peach in this recipe replaces unhealthy emotions with wisdom.

4 eggs, separated
½ cup sugar
¼ pint peach brandy
2 teaspoons rum or rum flavoring
¼ pint apple brandy
⅔ pint whole milk
¼ pint heavy cream
1 teaspoon vanilla extract

Directions: As you separate the eggs, visualize the negative energies being likewise separated from your partner. Using a hand mixer, beat the egg yolks and sugar together. When this thickens, add the remaining ingredients except the egg whites and vanilla. Chill.

Meanwhile, beat the egg whites until stiff. Fold these into the chilled egg mixture saying:

As I blend, healing I send
Into each cup, magick released as we sup!

Garnish cups with a fresh slice of apple or mint leaves (both of which have healthy energy). Sip, visualizing the liquid as white light that fills every cell and leaves no shadows where any problems can dwell.

Regeneration Grapes

The walnuts in this recipe replace stress with the ability to think things through clearly. That, combined with the healthy color and visionary vibrations of green grapes and the energy-heightening properties of ginger, makes for a great snack to inspire creative solutions to whatever's ailing your partner. The high water content of fruit also helps rehydrate your partner after a massage.

> *15–20 green seedless grapes (large)*
> *3 ounces softened cream cheese*
> *1 tablespoon crystallized ginger, finely chopped (or 1 tsp. powdered ginger)*
> *¼ cup very finely chopped walnuts*

Directions: Blend the cream cheese with the ginger, using a hand blender to "whip up" the energy. Roll each of the grapes in this mixture, turning them clockwise to coat them evenly, while saying:

> *Heal and renew, negativity abate*
> *In _____, good feelings create*

Insights restored, solutions to find
In these grapes, this magick I bind.

Chill the grapes in the freezer for 10 minutes. Meanwhile, spread out the walnuts on a piece of waxed paper. Roll the grapes in this powder so they're evenly coated. Chill again to likewise calm your emotions!

Banishing Garlic Dipping Oil & Bread

Persians trusted garlic to drive away evil spirits, as did many other ancient cultures. The red color of some of the garlic in this recipe helps keep away malicious spirits. Greeks offered this herb to Hecate, the goddess of magick. With that in mind, you'll be calling on Hecate for the magickal energy to banish the negatives in your partner's life.

3 large heads red or purple garlic, cut horizontally in half
1 clove elephant ear garlic, cut in half
3 cups virgin olive oil
4 sprigs thyme
1 teaspoon basil

Directions: Preheat the oven to 300 degrees. Put the garlic heads cut side down in a small casserole. Pour the olive oil over them. Add the thyme and basil evenly over top. (Note: if you want a more savory oil, you can also include sprigs of rosemary, marjoram, etc.) Cover with a lid or foil and bake, adding an incantation like this one:

> *Protective basil, garlic, and thyme*
> *Heed my will, Hecate hear my rhyme*
> *Drive away doubts and banish fears*
> *Only good energy may remain in here*

Bake for about 1 hour, until the garlic is soft enough to mash.

Mash the roasted garlic with a fork. Break up the whole herbs into similar-sized pieces (you can use a food processor or chopper for this, but finer is better). Store in an airtight container in the refrigerator for up to one month. Use in dishes such as soups, sauces, and stuffing.

Setting the Space

After you've completed the more mundane preparations for the massage, you'll want to turn your attention to the physical environment. If your mate is already tense or stressed, establishing a sacred space will help keep out unwanted interruptions and energies that might add to that stress.

Begin in the quarter of the room that represents your partner's area of need. For example, emotional distress comes under the water element, while physical distress and exhaustion are fire, financial and career stresses are earth, and mental or communication-caused stress are air. (You can refer back to Feng Shui Fantasies in Chapter 2 for more information about these elements.) By approaching the proper element first, you indicate its importance in what you're about to do. Your words need not be complex, but they should express the need you're trying to fulfill.

For illustrative purposes, let's say your partner has had a lot of frustrations at the office that are weighing heavily on his or her spirit. That would come under the realm of earth. Your invocation then might go something like this:

> *Welcome spirit of the Earth, who nourishes and gives us rich soil in which to grow. Come to this space to comfort _____(insert name) and bless him/her with renewed confidence at work.*

Ask the energy of that element into your sacred space to assist with the healing massage. You can also use the following invocations, depending on which energy you want to use.

> *Welcome spirit of the air, who gently blows with a fresh wind to aid our communications. Come to this space to comfort _____ (insert name), and bless this person with clarity of thought in his/her career.*

*Welcome spirit of fire, who warms our hearts and
shines a light in the darkness. Come to this space to
comfort_____(insert name), and bless him/her with
renewed energy for the tasks at hand.*

*Welcome spirit of the water, who cleanses, purifies,
and quenches our spirit's thirst. Come to this space to
comfort_____(insert name), and bless him/her with
healing from stress.*

When you're done with the invocation, light a
candle, or burn some incense to honor the energies
present.

You can also use affirmations that are focused on
healing and revitalization. Whispering words such as
relax, release, accept, and renew (in that order) become
a hypnotic mantra your partner can focus on. Eventually the conscious mind will start to release the stress
and chatter. End the massage with a prayer or blessing
to seal the energy.

sex pleasure in woman . . . is a kind of magic spell;
it demands complete abandon; if words or movements
oppose the magic of caresses, the spell is broken.

simone de beauvoir

5

Sweet Nothings

spells and charms for love and passion

Our ancestors weren't shy about using magick as a means to fulfill wishes, specifically in casting love spells. It's human nature to want to be loved and desired. This chapter outlines charms, amulets, and other simple spells that you can use in any relationship as the need arises. It also discusses gods and goddesses you can call upon in supporting those goals. A word of caution, however: Spells should never be devised in such a way as to force another's free will. When you're with someone, you want to know that he or she has made an honest choice to spend time with you (rather than having been "spelled" into it). Please keep that in mind when creating or adapting spells, or when using those provided.

Spellcraft Basics

In short, a spell is like a prayer to which you add other words, movements, and components that represent your intention. Rather than simply asking for something to happen, however, you change the energy around the situation to open the way for that manifestation or desired outcome.

Spells are driven by your will. Positive results in magick come from having a clear objective in your mind and being able to focus your thoughts on that goal entirely. In effect, you don't really need anything else for a spell to work, but "tools" such as crystals, herbs, or candles improve the sensual cues you receive. These sensual cues will in turn help you tap into the superconscious mind or Universal energies. Spiritual tools also help you get past the self and reconnect with spirit. Tools give you an emotional distance from the spell so you can stay on track. Rather than focusing on your self, your nervousness, your hopes, etc. Tools give you something else on which to focus along with your intent.

There are many different types of spellcraft. In this chapter, we'll explore charms and amulets, two of the most popular types of spells for attracting love and passion, as well as some methods adapted from ancient sources. Why were charms and amulets so popular? Because both are totally portable—talk about literally having magick in your pocket!

Charms and Amulets

From what history indicates, charms were the first forms of spells. Relatively simple to practice, they require nothing more than a verbalization to take effect. In fact, the word *charm* is derived from a word meaning "song" or "poem." Given that, it's not surprising that most charms are written in rhyme, giving them a lyrical quality. In addition, the rhyming cadence of most charms acts as a mnemonic device, so that whenever you need to recall the charm or spell it comes trippingly off the tongue without effort. That means you can put all of your attention on willful focus—rather than desperately trying to remember the words!

Later in history, when civilizations became a little more complicated, charms took on a different form. Words were still used, but an object or a bundle of objects, known as amulets, were added to help focus the intention or symbolize what the person casting the spell was trying to create. This is how we come by modern charm bracelets. With or without words, however, most charms focused their intentions on motivating positive energy—especially love, luck, physical prowess, and, of course, passion.

By comparison, amulets have a different intention. Amulets preserve or protect. They are carried to turn away the energies you do not want, and maintain those you do. An amulet's energy remains "off" until a situation calls that energy into action. For example, if you're carrying an amulet to keep the wrong people from approaching you at the bar, the amulet's energy will awaken when someone unwelcome tries to approach you. The result might be that the person decides to walk away, or that you have such a good comeback that they get your "back off" message loud and clear.

Remember that amulets will lose a bit of their energy each time they're used. Just as you need to recharge batteries, you'll need to recharge amulets periodically (traditionally by using the same method as originally instructed in the spell). For example, if the original spell called for repeating an incantation a set number of times, you'd hold the amulet and repeat that incantation the same number of times again. Or, if it called for leaving the amulet in the light of the moon for a set number of hours, you'd repeat that process. Unlike charms, amulets have always had a portable element. Typical components include stones, bones, pieces of metal, and herbs. We can certainly consider more modern components in our spell constructions, though, and you'll see ideas about that later in the book.

Before you launch into the spells themselves, it is often necessary to change a spell so that it's more meaningful to you or so the symbols make sense in terms of your goal. Think of the spells a bit like a recipe with which you can tinker. If you don't have the suggested components handy, find a substitute that maintains the continuity of the spell. For example, if a spell called for ginger ale because the bubbles encourage happiness, substituting club soda or berry-flavored soda would be fine. The first has the bubbles to lift your emotions; the second has berries, which inspire joy.

Remember that you can consider a component's color and aroma for symbolic value too. For example, if a spell called for tomato juice (tomatoes are called "love apples" in folk traditions) and you don't have any—how about something else that's red, or a heart-shaped stone perhaps? And don't stop with the ingredients—also ask yourself if the wording is comfortable for you, and whether you need to change the timing. While it takes a little creativity sometimes, you'll find the end result usually works better because of your efforts.

Sometimes you won't find a prefabricated spell. If that's the case, feel free to start from scratch and make your own. It's easier than you think. If you'd like some books to get you started, try these two books by Patricia Telesco: *Spinning Spells, Weaving Wonders* (Crossing Press) or *Magick Made Easy* (HarperSanFrancisco).

✳ The Spells ✳

For ease of reference, the spells in this section are set up alphabetically by their purpose or goal. For example, spells intended to deepen love come after those for encouraging a kiss (K precedes L). The spells included in this section are pretty straightforward and shouldn't contain any components or ingredients that you can't find in your home or on a supermarket shelf. Sexy sorcery doesn't have to have fancy components or overly complex processes to work effectively. Like any good witchery, it begins in the heart!

Attractiveness

Many people are their own worst critics. They look in the mirror and feel frumpy, ugly, or just plain yucky about themselves. This shouldn't be so! One important aspect to sensual sorcery is learning to celebrate the beauty within you—and then learning to share it with others.

May Day Dew-It

In European lore, the dew that's on the ground come May Day morning endows comeliness to those who wash their face in it. You can adapt this spell a bit by leaving out a large piece of cheesecloth the night before. In the morning, squeeze that water into a small dish. To this you might add a little rose water to increase the positive energies. Then dab the water on your face using an incantation like this one:

Let people see the inner me
With joy and light, my magick takes flight
And all will see, the magick is ME!

Accent the Positive

In Turkey, women wash their breasts with a mix of fenugreek seeds and water to make them grow. Adapting that a bit, you can use this blend to "grow" the best energies in your aura. To make the tincture, steep 1 cup of the herb in 5 cups alcohol (you can use any type of alcohol but many use vodka because it has no taste or aroma if they want to internalize the tincture). Put this in an airtight, dark jar. Shake this daily for a month while saying an incantation such as this:

The light within me, shine without
Remove my worries, remove my doubt
When this balm's applied to my skin
The magick's released, the spell begins.

You can apply this just before going into difficult social situations to boost your confidence.

Glamorous Aura

One way to give others the impression that you're very attractive and confident is by energizing your aura with those specific attributes. Because your aura completely surrounds your physical body, this spell, in effect, creates a glamorous atmosphere around you, and communicates that impression to all who look at you. You probably don't want to use this with people you care deeply about, because this spell creates a bit of an illusion. But to boost your confidence for a public mix-and-mingle, it can really help.

Begin by finding incense that matches your goal. To be more attractive to women, for example, try violet or patchouli. To be more attractive to men, try ginger or jasmine. Light the incense and put it in an incense holder in front of you. Now, take a feather or a hand-held fan and gently start moving that smoke into the air around your body (if it's easier, let it burn and walk through the smoke). As you do, visualize the energy of those herbs being absorbed by your body, making your aura glow brighter and more radiant. Add an incantation like this one:

> *Smoke of attraction, smoke of illusion, smoke of power*
> *Smoke raise energy, raise my image hour by hour*
> *So when people look at me,*
> *Only the very best will they see!*

Do this before any event, be it a first date, a job interview, a party, or anywhere you want to seem particularly attractive or alluring.

Erotic Energizing

Hoping the sun has gone down long before you and your mate get to sleep? Wishing that you and your mate had just a little more energy to enjoy an endless night of loving? Living in such a busy society, it's no wonder we're perpetually exhausted. After a full day of work, taking care of children, running errands, and balancing the checkbook, who couldn't use a little boost! Try some of these energizing spells.

Copal Copulation

Copal was a popular sacred herb among the Aztec, Incans, and Mayans. When blended with a pinch of frankincense and myrrh it's perfect for lighting a fire, just the way you want your body to be on fire when your lover touches you. For this spell you'll need a pinch of each of the three herbs and a safe fire source. Carry the herbs in a bundle with you all day, touching it each time you imagine what your lovemaking will be like later on. Savor those fantasies so the energy goes into the incense. Later, just before your mate arrives, put the incense in the burner and light it, saying:

Where this smoke touches let passion dwell
As the fire burns, so our bodies ignite with desire
Keep all weariness at bay, till dawn the new day!

Walk clockwise around the loving space with the incense and leave it somewhere safe to burn itself out.

Poppet Passion

In numerous cultures, small figurines of humans were used to direct energy to a specific individual. In this case, fashion some soft clay to represent you and your mate. You need not create a great work of art; however, your favorite pleasure center should dominate the finished work. As you're forming the poppet, focus on your goal and add repeated incantations like this one:

My body stays strong, all night long!

Put these in a safe place until after your lovemaking, and then return the clay to a neutral form to use another day.

Fantasy Poppet

Another way to use clay comes from an Egyptian tradition. Egyptians would gather clay from the Nile and make poppets, then bury them in the earth nearby, which was thought to have great restorative powers. Adapting this a bit, make your clay in the image of yourself. Take a toothpick and touch all the places where you want your body to tingle with desire when you and your mate are together. As you do, speak your fantasy into the doll, such as:

(touching the ears)
Let my body dance at the sound of your voice.
Speak to me of what we both desire.

Now, since you probably don't live near a riverbank, how about placing your poppet somewhere near your hearth (which represents "heat")? Keep it there until after your special night together, and then return it to neutral form.

Horseshoe Helpmate

The element of iron is associated with sexual power, especially in men; the crescent shape is feminine, symbolizing the moon's natural cycles and intuitive energy. To make the most of this combination, take out one ribbon that will represent you, and another that represents your lover. Tie these crisscross over an iron horseshoe and knot them at each crossing. Whisper your wishes for this partnering into each knot. Place this charm above your bed or the bedroom door with the opening downward to release its energy. Note that you will need to recharge this periodically by putting on fresh ribbons with new wishes attached!

Fertility (Pregnancy)

There are times when people will want their passionate encounters to have a long-term outcome, namely producing a child or children. There are many examples of fertility spells from around the world, but the following are the simplest and most easily adaptable for the novice.

Frog Fertility

The Zuni believed that frog spirits brought cleansing rain (water is a great fertility metaphor), and also helped with children. The latter association may have had something to do with the seemingly endless supply of tadpoles that come from frog eggs. Keeping an image of a frog in the bedroom and offering cornmeal to the frog spirit is said to be an excellent way to bless fertility.

In Western tradition, many find the image of a rabbit more suitable (an animal associated with the procreative nature). In this case, bring rabbit images and figurines into your loving space during the nights of the full moon for best results. The rabbit is associated with lunar energy, while the full moon represents completion or birth in a psychic sense.

Help from Astarte

The Semites honored Astarte as the goddess of love and fertility. Her symbol, the egg, bears testament to that association. She was also said to preside over aphrodisiacs. Among the aromatics associated with her are jasmine, rose, and myrrh. Use these as follows to create a fertility oil for yourself.

> ½ cup sweet almond oil
> 3 drops of each essential oil (one oil that represents you, one for your mate, and one for the child you hope to create)

Put the oils in a dark, airtight container. Dab a bit on your heart chakra and that of your partner before lovemaking. Also rub it into candles (before lighting) while saying:

Let our passion and love combine
in our bodies, in our minds
let this magick linger all the while
and produce within our wanted child

Sweet Sheets!

This idea comes from China, where people would put pieces of gold and silver, along with dates and chestnuts, on the newlyweds' bed to inspire fertility and wealth. We can adapt this idea, knowing that yellow is the color of the sun and conception, and silver is the color of the moon and the goddess. Dates and chestnuts also have strong masculine energy to balance out the female energies.

Prepare your loving space by leaving a bowl of dates and chestnuts in the loving space for snacking (even better—feed them to each other!). Make the bed using yellow and white or gold and silver sheets that have been dried with a bundle of fertility-oriented aromatics such as basil, lemon, rose petals, hibiscus, and/or apple. As you place the sheets on the bed, you can add an incantation like this one.

As I place these sheets, I open the way
to the spirit of love. Let it grow and blossom
and bring us a child. For the greatest good, so be it.

Happiness

Once you've found a partner you really click with, most likely you'll want to stay in that relationship and keep it upbeat and exciting. When you want to produce a little more levity and joy between you and your partner, try these spells.

Basil Bliss

Many cultures, including those of Greece and Rome, trusted basil to produce good feelings between people, including a sense of harmony. The easiest way to foster this energy is to simply keep basil plants in and around your loving space. As you put them where you wish, add an incantation such as this:

Leaves of happiness, roots filled with delight
Where your aroma floats, let this magick take flight!

Harmony Candle

In a variety of wedding rituals, lighting a single candle symbolizes unity. In this case, you'll be using that symbolism to make a special candle that honors the spirit of your home and all who dwell within.

To make the candle, you'll need a tall, thick, heat-proof glass holder (into which you'll pour the wax). You also need a wick that's long enough to reach the bottom of the glass, a small piece of foil, two candles (one chosen by you and one by your partner) and three aromatic oils (one chosen by each of you individually, and one agreed upon by both of you).

Melt the wax in a pan that you don't plan to use again for cooking. Let it cool, stirring it clockwise and adding the aromatic oils one drop at a time until you're happy with the scent. While it's cooling, suspend the wick in the glass by tying it to a pencil that you lay across the top. Put a small fold of aluminum foil on the bottom to weight the wick down in the center of the glass.

When you see the wax starting to lose its shininess, slowly pour it into the glass. Leave about ¾" at the top so you have a clean wick to light. Let the candle cool completely before using. Any time you feel as if stress or outside influences are disturbing your happiness, put this candle near your hearth (the heart of the home) and light it to improve the energies throughout the space. Let it burn for at least one hour for best results.

Wash Away Worries

Tension and worry are two things that can really dull passion and the joyfulness of a relationship. If you find that those types of feelings are overwhelming your space and communications, use the following method when you're cleaning the house.

First, make a mixture of baking soda and lemon rind, one cup baking soda with two tbs. lemon rind (finely ground) to sprinkle on the rugs. Let that sit in the rugs for a few minutes while you make wash water for the floors with lemon juice (I usually squeeze one lemon into a bucket for this purpose). Lemon has cleansing qualities and is also associated with love and joy. As you vacuum up the powder it will spread that fresh aroma around the house and gather up the negativity. As you wash the floors with the lemon-infused wash water, focus on washing away any energies you don't want. Then pour the dirty water down the toilet to flush your troubles away!

Healing

Every relationship goes through trials and tribulations. There are times when you'll hit a bump in the road with your partner. There are other times when relationships simply don't work out. In both instances, applying a magickal balm can go a long way toward making you feel whole and balanced again.

Healing a Broken Heart

This spell begins with any piece of fruit (an orange might be apt, as it represents devotion). Dice the fruit into small pieces. As you do, picture the fruit absorbing all of your anger and sadness. Now put it on a plate (covered to keep bugs away) and let it sit in the sun to rot. This natural decomposition process helps break down the negativity you're carrying. Finally, ritually bury or flush the fruit to likewise "put away" the past and let yourself begin anew.

Breaking the Ties that Bind

In Greek mythology, Ariadne (the daughter of King Minos) fell in love with the hero Theseus. However, Theseus was going to be sent into the labyrinth as an offering to the Minotaur. Ariadne cleverly gave Theseus a magic ball of thread, which led him to the Minotaur, which he killed, and then allowed him to find his way back out of the labyrinth safely. Though their story did not have a happy ending, Ariadne's interactions with Theseus helped her to eventually find true love. This spell builds on that story.

First you'll need an item that you can dispose of that represents the person with whom you've had a relationship. You also need some string. Tie the string around the item, then unwind enough so you have a free strand hanging off. Hold on to this free strand with one hand, and have scissors in the other. Say:

What was bound, I release
What was held in love, is returned in peace

As the cord is cut (snip the cord) and these words spoken
By my will, our bonds are broken

Note that this spell does not hurt you or the other person. It acknowledges the end of the relationship and releases your energy from each other and the union so that both of you can take your next step.

Forgiveness Spell

For this spell you'll need a medicinal balm (any kind). Everyone involved in the misunderstanding should come together and bring a candle. Have each person light his or her personal candle while saying:

With this light I bring peace. No ill will resides
in my heart
And through this spell, forgiveness impart.

It seems to work better if each person says the phrase while lighting the candle rather than doing so as a group. Once the candles are lit, whoever is leading this spell asks each person in turn, "Do you grant forgiveness freely and fully?" When everyone has answered in the affirmative, hold hands and chant:

Today's a new beginning
Today's a fresh start
Forgiveness is born in all of our hearts.

Blow out the candles in unison and ritually dispose of them to leave the past behind.

Renewal Charm

Every relationship needs a pick-me-up from time to time. If both you and your partner want to refresh the energies in your relationship, try making this charm. To begin, each of you should pick out small items that represent what you most want to bring to your relationship. For example, a small amethyst crystal could represent peace, while a dried flower can represent joy. Place each of these things, one by one, into a white pouch. Express your wishes to each other while looking into each other's eyes. Bundle up and hold the charm together, saying:

God/dess see our wishes and bless
Bring to us renewed happiness!

Keep the charm bag close to your hearth or in another place where you can see it often to remind you both of what you're working toward.

Kissing

Kissing is one of the most important preludes to passion. Kissing gets us aroused and actually helps adjust your aura to that of your mate's interest and energy levels. To help you stay kissable, get a box of candy breath mints and bless them all by saying:

A smile so full, and lips to lick
Come on now, and kiss me quick!

Keep these handy in the area where you plan to be snuggling. Even better, share one with your mate!

Love

Love is an amazing emotion. It seems to inspire both the best and worst in people because we feel it so very deeply. Ethically, it is best to cast love spells without a specific person in mind, or with someone who is already receptive to the energy.

Italian Amber Charm

This love spell comes from Italy. To start, you need a piece of amber. Wait until the night of a full moon. Go outside and hold the amber up to the light so you can look through it. As you do, think about all the things you desire in a potential lover or life mate. Be as specific as possible, and project those desires through the crystal toward the Universe.

That night, tuck the amber under your pillow. Keep it there all three nights of the full moon. Afterward, carry it in social situations to draw those who meet or exceed your desires.

Love Wish

This spell begins with a wishbone, so you'll need to clean and dry one from a chicken or turkey. Take three strands of your hair and braid them around the wishbone (one for you, one to bring a person into your life, and one for your union together). As you cross each strand, say words that describe your dream mate. Examples may include passionate, loving, kind, tall, dark, gentle, creative, fun, and so on. Put this carefully in a red bag or cloth (red symbolizes love) and set it out beneath the full moon, or beneath the first star that appears in the night sky, until your wish manifests. At that point, bury the bundle so that love can grow.

Petal Power

Take a handful of pink and red rose petals. Pink represents the initial friendship necessary for love to grow, and red is for the actual romantic love. Wait until dawn (the time of hope) and go outside your home or apartment. Hold these in your hand and think about the kind of person you would want for a romantic relationship. Then sprinkle the petals on the pathway leading to your door so that love "follows" you home! Keep any extra petals to use in love incense or charms.

Marriage

I have been fortunate to preside over several magickal marriage ceremonies. It's a wonderful experience to watch as energies mix, mingle, and slowly weave two people into one life. Marriage spells are designed to support that union before, during, and after the ceremony.

Keep an Eye on Things

In Europe, it wasn't uncommon for one or more of the bridal party members to carry an eye agate with them. This is a stone that looks distinctly like an eye in shape and coloring, and it was considered a very potent talisman against the "evil eye" (or anyone who did not hold the best wishes in their heart for the union). In a magickal ritual, this stone can be placed on the altar "looking" outward at those gathered. Bless it before the ritual, saying:

> *Eyes be keen, eyes be sure*
> *I bless you with magick, pure*
> *Keep all ill will and thoughts at bay*
> *Grant us blessings this special day.*

Delight Ducks

Another symbol that showed up in many engagement parties and wedding rituals was a pair of ducks. It is said that ducks mate for life, and thus they symbolize devotion and fidelity. Rather than placing these on the altar, consider using these in the reception hall along with orange blossoms to protect your love and inspire harmony. Energize these charms with an incantation like this one:

Birds of a feather now live together
In trust and love, blessed from Above
And in wedded bliss, sealed with a kiss!

Wishing Trees

In Celtic regions, people would often take snippets of cloth and other items and tie them to trees while reciting their wish or desire. When the item loosed itself in the wind, the wish "winged" its way toward fulfillment. You can do something similar at a wedding reception. Give each person a ribbon, and place a live, miniature tree near the couple. Attendees can come up throughout the reception and speak their wish as they tie the ribbons. The couple then takes this tree home and only unties one ribbon at a time as they have a need. Note that one ribbon should always remain on the tree to represent the ongoing vitality of the relationship.

Divine Helpmates

People around the world have turned to deities who preside over friendship, love, and companionship to aid them with their relationships. By focusing on an aspect of the Divine that you're drawn to, and that represents the assistance you most need, you can improve the overall energies with which you have to work in your sensual sorcery. For example, if you're looking for romantic love, it makes sense to call on the goddess Venus for assistance.

Having said that, however, one does not simply "command" Divine assistance. You need to build a relationship with specific Beings before asking for aid. Remember to pronounce each name correctly, and have something in the sacred space to honor him or her. This is simply respectful, and gives you a much better feeling for the powers with which you're planning to work on an intimate level.

Here's just a brief list of gods and goddesses for your consideration. There are certainly hundreds more from many pantheons from which you could choose (depending on your goal) if you don't find something suitable here. Books such as *Encyclopedia of Gods* by Michael Jordan (Facts on File, Inc., 1993) can help in your searches. The following is an abbreviated list of gods and goddesses you can call upon to help with love, pleasure, fertility, and commitment:

Adonis (Greek): God of physical attributes, especially strength, health, and vigor

Agni (Hindu): God of fire and fertility

Ahsonnutli (Navajo): Bisexual god figure

Ama No Uzume (Japanese): Goddess of erotic dance, temptation, playfulness, and fertility

Anagke (Greek): Goddess of destiny and meeting needs

Anahita (Persian): Women's goddess of marriage and childbirth

Anat (Canaanite): mistress of all gods; the goddess of love and fertility

Aphrodite (Greek): Goddess of sex, beauty, love, and passion

Apollo (Greek/Roman): God of fertility, honesty, and effective communication

Aramati (Hindu): Goddess of dedication and fidelity

Arani (Hindu): Goddess of erotic energy, sexual fire, and alternative sexual lifestyles.

Atergatis (Syrian): Goddess of wisdom and procreation

Bacchus (Greek): God of teasing, playfulness, fertility, wine, ecstasy, and jubilation

Bast (Egyptian): Goddess of pleasure, happiness, youthful joy, sensuality, and sex

Belit-Ilanit (Chaldean): Goddess who brings people into harmony; also the goddess of eroticism

Bullai-Bullai (Aborigine): Goddess who helps star-crossed lovers find their way

Cupid (Roman): God of erotic love, who brings people together

Dahud (Breton): Goddess of uninhibited passion and magnetism

Devi (Indian): Goddess of inventive sexual interaction

Dionysus (Greek): God of fecundity and ecstacy

Eos (Greek): Goddess of young love and desire

Eros (Greek): God of erotic love and all types of relationships

Erzulie (Haitian Voodoo): Goddess who fixes things between lovers

Fand (Irish): Goddess of loving pleasure

Fides (Roman): Goddess of faithfulness, devotion, and upright intentions

Freya (Teutonic): Goddess who protects sacred unions

Hawthor (Egyptian): Goddess of sensuality, unrestrained eroticism, and beauty

Hera (Greek): Goddess of women, marriage, childhood, and the "perfect" relationship

Hotei (Japanese): God of laughter and joy

Hulda (Teutonic): Goddess of fertility and marriage

Inanna (Sumerian): Goddess of sacred unions

Indrani (Hindu): Goddess of magnetism and satisfaction

Kara (Teutonic): Goddess of charisma, also a valkyrie, some believe her story eventually became sleeping beauty

Kwan Yin (Chinese): Goddess of compassion and fecundity

Lakshmi (Hindu): Goddess of attractiveness, joie de vivre, and good luck.

Liban (Irish): Goddess of happiness and pleasure

Meni (Chaldean): Goddess of fated love

Min (Egyptian): God of sexual aptitude

Nanan-Bouclou (Benin): Bisexual god

Nunakawa-Hime (Japanese): Goddess of negotiation and wisdom in relationships

Ogun (Nigerian): God of lovers

Oshun (Nigerian): Goddess of lush beauty, pleasing dress, and rich aromatics

Priapus (Greek): Phallic god who presides over fertility

Rakshasis (Hindu): Goddess of attraction and charm

Rati (Hindu): Goddess of passion and sexual pleasure

Sjofna (Teutonic): Goddess of all forms of love

Sradda (Hindu): Goddess of assurance and conviction

Tara (Tibetan): Goddess of love, compassion, and eroticism

Tvashtar (Hindu): God of enthusiasm and stimulation

Xochipilli (Aztec): God of love, lovers, and marriage

Yarilo (Slavonic): God of sexual love, fertility, and passion

Whether or not you choose to work with a Divine Being, spells are a great addition to your sensual sorcery with but one caveat: Don't attempt to force or manipulate love, because you will always wonder about that relationship's veracity (should it survive) in the future. In any relationship, be it short term or long term, honoring the person you're with as a Sacred Being is very sexy, and results in far more interesting and mutual encounters.

*there is no love sincerer
than the love of food.*

george bernard shaw

Sexy Servings

the food and drink of love

ood has long been a part of magick and sexy sorcery. That's not particularly surprising when you consider that food engages all of the senses: sight, smell, taste, touch, and yes, even hearing. (Think about hearing the sizzle of food cooking on the stove, or the fizz of champagne and sparkling beverages. Aphrodisiacs—foods reputed to induce sexual desire—have long been a part of witchery.

Various cultures have different lore and traditions surrounding magickal food. In ancient times, people distinguished between foods and beverages that increased fertility and the ones that simply increased sex drive, both of which were important in that they worked together for human goals. Nonetheless, the preoccupation with aphrodisiacs may have arisen from necessity. One of the key issues in earlier times was malnutrition (the knowledge of what made for a good diet simply didn't exist, and there weren't any 24-hour stores). This created certain vitamin deficiencies that, in turn, produced libido loss, decreased fertility, and/or increased infant mortality rates.

Symbolically speaking, substances that by nature looked like seed or semen, such as egg whites, were assumed to have inherent sexual properties for men especially (the law of similars again). Other types of foods, like the banana, were considered stimulating because of their physical resemblance to genitalia. Ancient Greeks, among many other earlier cultures, identified and documented these foods as seemed locally accurate, and it's this material to which we still often turn in modern times for reference purposes.

Mythology also played a role in determining which foods held potential for meeting the magickal needs of early humankind. For example, Aphrodite, the goddess of love, considered sparrows sacred. They're considered very loving birds by observational standards; thus, a sparrow might be tried in an aphrodisiac brew or food. Agreed—ewww! But we can't randomly judge the ancients by our modern knowledge or social structure. Remember that these people were, for the most part, less educated and far more superstitious.

The list of items that the ancients tried was fairly extensive (a number of them are listed for you in Chapter 1), because our ancestors—not unlike ourselves—wanted to feel attractive, passionate, and sexually adequate, if not downright astounding! A great deal of this mythology and folklore remains with us and influences the way we continue to use foods in modern times. The recipes in this chapter build on that repository by taking specific ingredients and blending them together for the best possible energies.

Lovin' in the Oven

The Americans have always been
food, sex, and spirit revivalists.
Edward Dahlberg

The recipes in this section, which are set up by key ingredient, expand upon what you learned in Chapter 1. As you're preparing any of these recipes, or those of your own creation, remember to add spiritual touches. Cooking is already a mini-ritual that most people approach with personal flair and a hint of tradition. You're just taking that mini-ritual to new levels.

Please don't think this requires redoing your kitchen so it looks like a magazine picture, or that you need to be a fabulous culinary artist. That's absolutely not the case. However, what it does require is purposeful focus. Rather than just strolling into your kitchen and tossing ingredients together, you're now using this area as a sacred space in which you're going to build a specific type of energy. Definitely don't cook sexy servings when you're angry, sick, or stressed. Those are the last types of energy any sexy sorceress wants in foods!

One thing that is helpful is taking a hot aromatic shower or minimally washing your hands with some specially chosen soap (kept only for these occasions) before you prepare magickal foods. This is good from a health perspective, of course, but it also reminds you that you're doing something important, something out of the ordinary. That mental connection begins the mini-ritual. You'll probably have to experiment a bit to see what puts you in the best state of mind for making magickal menus.

In addition to a positive attitude, bring all your metaphysical know-how into the kitchen. For instance, consider having a hearth candle ready for this type of work. A hearth candle is one specifically designed to honor whatever facet of the Divine you choose for your kitchen (or, if you prefer, to honor the Great Spirit as a whole). We see customs like this around the world, in places as far removed as Japan, where something was kept near the stove to commemorate and welcome the Divine. It's a lovely custom. You can fine-tune this practice by placing a symbol that represents a passionate god or goddess who can support your magickal goals. To do this, dab the candle with an aromatic that represents that Being, or carve his or her name into the candle. Just remember to continue the relationship-building process with that deity (see Chapter 5).

Also, how about prepping your ingredients during auspicious astrological times? You also can stir things clockwise to attract positive energy, and counterclockwise to banish negativity. Chant, sing, or pray over your foods, telling the Universe what you most want and need. Burn symbolic incense or play New Age music. Most important, visualize energy pouring into each drop and morsel of food, and consume with an expectant heart.

You'll find that only a few of the many aphrodisiac foods and components are covered in this chapter. You'll also notice that some recipes blend the best of the individual components into meaningful and powerful sensual edibles. Please let both the stories of the ingredients, the recipes themselves, and your own imaginative taste buds inspire many more creative ideas of your own. Don't be afraid to tinker and do more research into the foods of love. If you're aware of a recipe from a family tradition that's meant to inspire sexual sorcery, by all means try it! The familiarity and special nature of that dish helps support your magickal goals.

Asparagus

Chinese herbalists used asparagus to treat everything from infertility to joint aches and pains. Frenchmen of the nineteenth century swore that eating three courses of asparagus on the night before their wedding would improve performance. Interestingly enough, the vitamins in asparagus do seem to improve hormone production. For best results, feed your lover lightly boiled or steamed spears at least three times that day (don't overboil, or you'll lose a lot of good vitamins).

From a health perspective, asparagus is high in folic acid, vitamin C, potassium, and beta carotene (all of which support the immune system).

Zealous Asparagus (2 servings)

The lemon in this dish provides two types of energy, the first being love and devotion and the second being zest (both literally and figuratively!).

> 1 pound asparagus, tough ends trimmed
> ½ tablespoon unsalted butter
> ½ tablespoon lemon juice
> ½ tablespoon lemon zest (fresh; if you want more
>   devotion, use orange)
> salt and pepper to taste

Directions: Cook asparagus in a wide 6-quart pot of boiling water (or if you have a vegetable steamer, that's a very nice way to prepare fresh asparagus). It takes about 7 minutes of boiling or 10 minutes of steaming for the vegetables to become tender. Drain the asparagus and toss with butter, lemon or orange, and salt and pepper (let your movements carry your intentions into the dish!).

Serving Suggestion: Sprinkle a mixture of Italian cheese on top of this dish. Cheese is another love food, it keeps the asparagus hot, and it adds a lovely flavor.

Dragon Tales (Asparagus with Tarragon) (4 servings)

The word *tarragon* means "little dragon," which speaks of the bold flavor of this herb. When you want your sensual energy to be as long-lived as the ancient dragons were said to be, try this dish!

> 1½ pound medium asparagus, trimmed (the thinner the asparagus, the better)
> ½ tablespoon white wine vinegar
> ½ tablespoon balsamic or cider vinegar
> 2 teaspoons minced shallot (or garlic and onions combined)
> ¼ teaspoon Dijon or other coarse ground mustard
> ⅛ teaspoon kosher salt
> ⅛ teaspoon black pepper

3 tablespoons olive oil
sesame oil (dash)
1½ teaspoons finely chopped fresh tarragon
1 large egg, hard-boiled (optional—good for fertility)

Directions: Steam the asparagus until tender (about 5 to 7 minutes). Cool and drain. In a separate bowl, using a wire whisk, blend the vinegar and all of the rest of the ingredients except the egg. Slice the egg lengthwise four times. Put the asparagus on four plates, top each serving with a slice of egg, and drizzle the dressing over top.

Serving suggestion: If you wish, you can use a toothpick to draw a symbol of your desire in the egg, so that the energy "hatches" afterward!

Crab

In Pacific regions, crab is eaten regularly as an aphrodisiac. Nutritionally, crabmeat is an excellent source of high-quality protein, vitamins, and minerals that are needed for energy and a vigorous, happy sex life. Crabmeat is also an excellent source of phosphorus, zinc, copper, calcium, and iron and is very low in fat, especially saturated fat, making it perfect for lovers who are watching their diets to make themselves healthier and more appealing to each other.

Curing Crabby Attitudes (2 servings)

Ever gone through one of those weeks where you and your mate seem to be sniping at each other constantly? If so, this dish is a great place to start fixing things. The law of sympathy tells us that like affects like—meaning that by cracking the crab shells, you're showing power over that negative attitude (and the firm intention to put it in the past). The bacon grounds your intention with real action, and the tomato brings loving words and action back "online." As an aside, once you're over being angry, the crabmeat may inspire a little passion as a bonus!

4 large fresh tomatoes (with flat bottoms)
extra-virgin olive oil
½ pound crabmeat flakes (real or imitation)
1 egg, beaten
½ small white onion, minced (white for peace)
1 stalk celery, finely chopped
2 tablespoons butter
1 cup seasoned-style bread crumbs
dash salt and pepper
2 teaspoons crumbled bacon bits (optional)
2 tablespoons balsamic vinaigrette

Directions: Carefully slice off the top of the tomatoes and scoop out the meat (you can set this aside for a salad, soup, or sauce in the future). Rub the tomatoes inside and out with olive oil, then put them bottom down in an ovenproof, oiled pan. Next, mix the crab-meat with the beaten egg and set aside.

In a frying pan, gently sauté the onions and celery in butter until the onions are golden brown. Add this to the crab along with the bread crumbs and salt and pepper to taste. Scoop this mixture into the tomatoes. Bake at 350 degrees for 25 minutes. Place in the center of two serving dishes, sprinkled with bacon bits and surrounded by the vinaigrette if you so choose.

Serving suggestion: If you have two blue plates they'll emphasize your efforts, because blue is the color of peace. Alternatively, any touches of yellow on the table, such as yellow flowers, will improve communication. For those who do not enjoy tomatoes, you can substitute red peppers in this dish (red emphasizing loving intentions).

Crazy Crab (2 servings)

In many coastal regions, especially those of the Pacific, it is said that crab served with coconut doubles the passionate power of the meal (wow!). This recipe also has hot pepper to liven things up and keep them sizzling. The flavors are rich together, and you and your partner can serve each other pieces of this by hand for a more romantic flair.

⅓ cup unsweetened coconut milk (the fresher the better!)
3 green onions, diced

1 teaspoon red pepper flakes
½ cup mayonnaise or generic white salad dressing
3 tablespoons fresh lime or lemon juice
1 pound jumbo crab meat, in small chunks

Directions: Place all ingredients but the crab in a mixing bowl. Whisk thoroughly until well combined. Chill this for a few hours, then serve the crab with toothpicks for dipping. If you wish, you can warm the crab briefly in a sauté pan to heat things up to the next level.

Serving suggestion: Using a teaspoon, dab a little of the dip on plates in the shape of a heart with the crabmeat in the center!

Ginger

Ginger root is a circulatory system stimulant that adds flavor and energy to any meal. Because ginger increases blood circulation, it improves the sensitivity in your body's erogenous zones (not to mention helping alleviate cold hands and feet in bed). Candied ginger is a wonderful way to finish a passionate meal and make you more kissable!

Healthwise, ginger warms internal organs, eases depression, and cures ailments from colds to nausea. It's high in vitamins A and C, has concentrated antioxidants, and naturally supports your immune system.

Sassy Ginger Sauce (yields approx. 2—3 cups)

This sauce makes for very sassy and sexy energies by combining orange (love and devotion), ginger (energy and passion), honey (sweet joy and fertility if you so desire), and passion fruit (lust). Use it over a giant vanilla ice cream sundae for two, with sliced bananas for more symbolic potency.

> ½ cup passion fruit or pomegranate juice
> ¼ cup orange juice (fresh if possible)
> 2 tablespoons orange blossom honey
> 1 tablespoon ginger pulp (or finely ground candied ginger)
> 2 ounces diced apricot (dried or fresh)
> 2 passion fruit, scooped

Directions: Cook all but the passion fruit in a saucepan over a low flame for about 5 minutes. While that cooks, scoop the pulp of one fruit and add it to the pan. Cook for 5 minutes more until apricots are tender. Cool and place in a blender and purée for smoothness (symbolically making for smooth interactions). Add the chunks of the remaining fruit to this, and serve in dessert dishes.

Serving suggestion: I like to top this with whipped cream, but be forewarned that you may end up wearing it (and becoming dessert yourself)!

Slice of Life Pie (6—8 servings)

This is a great pie to make in fall or winter as comfort food that warms up both body and soul. The pumpkin provides protective energies for your relationship, while the ginger and sugar keep things upbeat and enthusiastic, especially when you need a boost.

> 1 9" pre-prepared pie crust (graham cracker is the best)
> 1 15-ounce can pure packed pumpkin
> ½ cup (packed) brown sugar
> ⅓ cup orange blossom honey
> 3 large eggs
> 1¼ cups whipping cream (flavored, if desired)
> 1 tablespoon finely grated peeled fresh ginger
> 1 teaspoon ground cinnamon
> 1 teaspoon vanilla extract or vanilla powder
> Whipped cream or ice cream (garnish)

Directions: Mix pumpkin, sugar, and honey in large bowl. Whisk in eggs one at a time, followed by cream, ginger, cinnamon, and vanilla. Pour into crust. Bake pie until set, covering edges with foil collar if browning too fast, about 60 minutes. Cool. Garnish as desired.

Prep note: You can use a rune or other symbol in the pie crust to "bake in" the magick!

Honey

The therapeutic aspects of honey have been known for about 5,000 years. When taken in small daily doses, it acts as an overall elixir for the body. Honey improves our energy, which is why many athletes use it in their diets. Even the ancient Olympians enjoyed it daily.

Voracious Salad (2 servings)

The honey in this dish strengthens male virility with vitamin B and nitric oxide. The nuts add zinc and amino acid to stimulate blood flow to "hot spots," and the cheese tops off the dish with a little smooth energy and love so your passionate hunger cannot be denied!

12 whole romaine lettuce leaves
12 whole red cabbage leaves (or red lettuce for
    passion)
2 tablespoons soft blue cheese or gorgonzola
1 teaspoon honey
12 walnuts
1 tablespoon softened butter (optional)

Directions: Make sure the cheese and honey are at room temperature. Mix these together in a bowl with the softened butter. Gently dice up the walnuts. Put a bit of cheese mix into each leaf, sprinkle in walnuts, and roll up as you would a stuffed grape leaf. Place these on a plate with a little extra honey as a garnish. Feed them expectantly to each other. *After-snack idea:* Dust each other with honey powder (which can be found at most adult stores) and get creative!

Marry-Me Mead

In Teutonic tradition, the goddess Freya's name meant "well-beloved," an indicator of what a valuable wife-partner she was to Odin. Freya protected marriages and fertility; her partner Odin presided over matters including skill, magickal arts, and poetry. They certainly made a very romantic pair! The following recipe is equally romantic, because mead was often given to couples on their honeymoon.

Strawberries are among the sacred fruits of Freya, representing earth's bounty, and inspiring gentle love with their pink-red hue. The honey in mead is perfect for inspiring the muse when you wish to speak to your beloved with sweet words.

> 1 pound frozen strawberries in juice
> 1 16-ounce can frozen strawberry daiquiri juice
>   concentrate
> 1 gallon water
> 1 quart heather honey (or orange blossom, which
>   inspires devotion)
> ½ package champagne yeast (can be found at brewing
>   supply shops and some super-supermarkets)

1 orange, sliced
1 orange pekoe tea bag

𝒟*irections:* Consider making this blend when the moon is in the waxing-to-full phase so the mead ages properly, and so your love "waxes" likewise full! Place all of your ingredients except the yeast in a non-aluminum pan over medium heat. Allow the mead to come to a low rolling boil. As it does, some scum from the honey will rise to the top. Skim this off. As you do, add an incantation like this one:

Freya, goddess of love so sweet
Aid my quest—make love complete
Upon my lips warm, gentle words
Let this prayer and need be heard

Continue this way for one hour; then let the mead cool to lukewarm.

Meanwhile, place the yeast in ¼ cup of warm (*not* hot) water, and stir. Let this set until the mead has cooled properly. Strain out the berries, teabag, and orange slices, and then blend the yeast mixture into the mead. Cover the pot with a heavy towel to steep for one week (you'll know all is well if bubbles have formed on the surface within 24 hours). Strain again, pouring the clearest liquid into bottles. Lightly cork the bottles and keep them in a cool, dark room for two months. After this, you can pour off the clearest liquid one last time, and bottle with tight-fitting corks.

Allow this to age for a full year and a day before serving. Share this at weddings, anniversaries, engagements, or romantic interludes for warm results. It's especially effective if served from one common cup to symbolize unity of mind and heart. In a hurry? Get a bottle of mead at a beverage store and serve it warm with a strawberry garnish!

Olives and Olive Oil

The curative properties of olives and olive oil have been known for a long time, which is why the Mediterranean diet has proved to be very healthy! Symbolically speaking, we can't ignore the image of an olive branch as representing success (the Olympic games) and a cease to any hostilities (make love, not war!).

Greek Gods' Rice (4—5 one cup servings)

The Greek gods and goddesses were known to be a passionate lot. Perhaps it was because their food had all the right energies to encourage a little playful zeal! This dish combines the sacred food of Athena (olives) with tomatoes and feta to make you a god or goddess in your own bedroom. Rice inspires fertility or virility, depending on what you desire. Better still, it's fast and easy, leaving more time for love!

2 cups long grain or brown rice
1 cup diced canned tomatoes in basil and garlic
½ cup sliced black (or green) olives
1 cup feta cheese
butter and olive oil

$\mathcal{D}$*irections:* Rinse the rice before cooking. When light and fluffy, toss in the tomatoes and olives. Scoop out to the plate, adding a slice of fresh butter on top surrounded by feta cheese.

Serving suggestions: Why not treat each other like deities and feed each other, one sexy spoonful at a time!

$\mathcal{L}$*uscious* $\mathcal{O}$*live* $\mathcal{S}$*pread (yield: 1½ cups)*
The olives in this dish provide a peaceful foundation between two people; the walnuts offer conscious wisdom of your partner's needs and wants; and the herbs and pepper add a little spice to keep things tempestuous!

1¾ cups pitted cured black olives (about ½ pound
   pitted)
¼ cup walnuts, toasted, chopped
¼ cup virgin olive oil
2 teaspoons Dijon mustard

1 garlic clove, whole

1 teaspoon chopped fresh thyme

1 teaspoon chopped fresh oregano

1 teaspoon chopped fresh sage

Pinch of cayenne pepper

Directions: Finely chop the black olives. Add the olive oil, Dijon mustard, garlic, thyme, oregano, sage, and cayenne pepper into a blender or food processor and purée (don't let this get too mushy, however; you want a little texture). Stir in chopped toasted walnuts. Chill and serve as part of finger sandwiches, or with vegetables or crackers as a dip.

Adaptations: Try this with honey mustard and regular black or green olives for minor taste variations. The honey adds that aphrodisiac energy, and green olives promote growth or new beginnings, whereas black olives are more foundational (earthy).

Roses

Roses bring emotional balance into lovemaking. They have a natural aromatic ability to help us heal on a physical and emotional level. Beyond this, the uplifting energy of this queen of flowers makes it much sought after as an aphrodisiac and antidepressant.

Ravish-Me Fruit Salad (6 servings)

Roses represent love and marriage. They've been given as a gift between lovers for thousands of years. Even Cleopatra used roses to woo Mark Antony! Here we combine the aroma and taste of roses with fruit, a symbol of earth's bounty and happiness. Specifically, oranges inspire devotion; strawberries, love; and raspberries, playful joy.

1½ cups water

½ cup vanilla sugar (available in stores, or make it yourself by putting a whole vanilla bean in your sugar canister)

1 cinnamon stick, broken in half

2 teaspoons rose water

4 oranges

2 cups red grapes, halved

½ pint strawberries, halved

½ pint raspberries

1 pear, cored and sliced

Directions: Stir the water and sugar in a heavy medium saucepan over low heat until sugar dissolves. Increase heat to medium-high. Add cinnamon and stir slowly while bringing the mixture to a boil. Let this reduce down to one cup of syrup (this takes about 10 minutes). Peel the oranges and separate them. Add the remaining fruit to the syrup. Blend with syrup and chill for two hours before serving.

Serving suggestion: Rather than whipped cream, try this with just a drizzle of sweet cream on top (remember to pattern it creatively!).

Sandwiched in Love

The Romans used roses to mark life's most important occasions, including weddings. Persian warriors are said to have adorned their shields with red roses for protection, and in the Middle Ages, lovers would often have trysts in a rose garden to safeguard their secret! These little sandwiches surround rose petals in a womb of bread, for earthy energy.

2 sourdough bread slices, toasted
One large leaf of romaine lettuce
10 large rose petals (best picked fresh)
½ cup goat cheese, softened
¼ cup pine nuts, chopped
Red onion slices
½ cup plain yogurt
½ teaspoon rose water

Directions: Wash the lettuce and rose petals (these should be organic and as fresh as possible!). Place the lettuce on one slice of the toasted bread. On top, spread the goat cheese, sprinkle the pine nuts, then place the rose petals so they evenly cover the surface. Add onion slices. Set aside for a moment.

Mix the yogurt with the rose water and use this as a dressing. You can either put the other slice of bread on top and cut into finger sandwiches, or serve as two open-faced sandwiches.

Adaptation: Try this with strawberry yogurt to enhance loving energy.

Tomatoes

I love them, the love apple . . . the best way to eat them is in the garden, warm and pungent from the vine.
M. F. K. Fisher from With Bold Fork and Knife

The tomato is both a fruit and an herb and is rich in vitamins A and C, so you can build up substantial physical energy for your date. It comes by its reputation as a love food in two ways: the rich red color has a strong association with matters of the heart, and the French name for tomato is *pomme d'amour*—the apple of love. And anyone who's had a French lover knows that they celebrate their passionate foods, and their foods with a passion!

The Italians were among the first to actively cultivate tomatoes, and it seems they had more in mind than simple soup and salads. I remember as a child standing in an elder Italian woman's kitchen as she carefully blended tomatoes into a savory sauce. She hummed a little tune, smiled knowingly, and said "That will fix it!" I asked, somewhat confused (as nothing seemed broken), "Fix what?" She laughed, sounding a bit like gentle bells, and replied, "Ah, this heals broken hearts and brings lovers back together—guaranteed!" It seems that heart-healing tomato sauce is an old tradition in many Strega homes! When cooking with tomatoes, remember that while we think of it as a vegetable, it has the characteristics and potential sweetness of fruit. This, in turn, makes the energies likewise sweet and pleasant. From that foundation, you can build a dish with as much spice (naughty or nice) as you wish!

Forgiveness Fried Tomatoes

Basil is an herb known for improving the rapport between lovers and cooling over-heated tempers. The Catalina-style dressing here likewise encourages reconciliation by smoothing the way toward understanding.

> *1 egg*
> *1 cup water*
> *1 teaspoon freshly diced basil (more if you wish)*
> *1 teaspoon salt*
> *1 cup all purpose flour*
> *1 cup beer (room temperature)*
> *2 large tomatoes*
> *salt and pepper*
> *Olive oil*
> *Catalina dressing*

Directions: Beat the egg and water together. Slowly add the basil, salt, flour, and beer until well incorporated. Set aside for one hour. In the meantime, slice the tomatoes crosswise at half-inch intervals. Sprinkle with salt and fresh ground pepper. Pat dry before dipping in the batter. Heat a large frying pan, covering the bottom with about ¼" of olive oil. Fry the batter-dipped tomatoes on both sides until golden brown. Lay out on a serving platter with a drizzle of Catalina dressing.

Serving suggestion: Most salad dressing bottles have a control-top lid that will allow you to actually write your intention on this dish. Words like "I'm sorry" or "Wanna make up?" are a good start!

Topping alternative: Rather than the salad dressing, sprinkle blue cheese or feta cheese with a drizzle of balsamic vinegar. Magickally speaking, cheese inspires love and devotion, and the vinegar keeps things spicy!

Salsa Soup

This delightfully simple dish is definitely for those occasions when you want to start out your meal with a bang. The salsa here provides lots of fiery energy, delicately offset by the cheese for a passion driven by pure love.

1 10-ounce can tomato soup (smooth)
10 ounces medium-hot salsa

Sour cream
Cheddar cheese (shredded)

Directions: Follow the instructions on the soup can for adding water. Blend in the salsa and let this mixture cook over a low flame for 20 minutes so that the soup accepts the flavoring fully. Pour into bowls, placing a dollop of sour cream in the center of each. Sprinkle cheddar cheese on top (in the shape of a heart) and serve hot.

Serving suggestions: Serve this dish with warm pita in the light of red, cinnamon-scented candles. Also consider using pineapple salsa in this dish. The sweetness matches that of the tomatoes, and pineapple represents hospitality, making for an even cozier evening!

Kitchen Project

This is a fun thing to try in your home, and it will change the way you look at food forever. Go into your kitchen and make a list of all the edible items you have (don't forget spices!). Using Chapter 1 as a reference, see how many of them are already considered a "food of love" that you could use in magickal cooking. Also, how many of these foods have loving or passionate associations for you personally?

When time allows, do some research on the folklore behind the items on your list to see what other types of metaphysical energy they contain. Also, make your own notes about the personal meanings these foods have for you. Use this list in the future to help you prepare any sexy serving or pantry enchantment. Better yet, you can pull together a collection of your own sexy recipes and give them to your beloved as a gift.

What foods you resonate to as sensual will be highly personal and subjective. Here's a sample of some items on my personal list:

+ Wine vinegar—the red color has associations with love; the snappy taste provides energy and clarity
+ Peanut butter (crunchy)—the nuts are a natural symbol of male testes
+ Unrefined sugar—sweetness, but not sickly sweet, for well-grounded love and happiness
+ Cream soup—the smoothness connotes harmony

These examples give you an idea of what I see as personal meanings in some items I regularly use in cooking. Think about it a little. Pretty soon the magickal potential of everything in your home will begin to jump out at your senses, and help you with your sorcery!

*all earthly delights are sweeter in expectation
than in enjoyment; but all spiritual pleasures
more in fruition than in expectation.*

francois de salignac fenelon

Foreplay

daring divinations and
romantic rituals

he previous chapter explored cooking as a mini-
ritual, one that is often steeped in family or
cultural traditions and memories. Cooking, however,
certainly isn't the only ritual in life. Take, for example,
the child's game of picking daisy petals while saying
"loves me, loves me not." That's a ritual. It's also a type
of spell and divination! Or, what about dating? There
are certainly a variety of social rituals and customs that
go with "wooing," such as gifts, wining and dining, and
exchanging phone numbers and astrological signs. So
you see, ritual is a part of everyday life—you just haven't
been doing it consciously. This chapter examines various types of divination and rituals you could practice

before going out, while having a romantic dinner, or just while spending time with your partner, to help make sensual adventures more successful.

Fantasies and Fortunetelling

There are many junctures in a relationship when all of us wish we had a little more perspective, be it wondering whether or not to make that first date or thinking about long-term commitments. Sometimes we just can't separate our hopes and dreams from what's realistic. Other times we get so down on ourselves or stressed about our lovers that we couldn't recognize something good if it bit us! Both of these types of situations are ones in which using divination could be very helpful. Divination tools provide you with some emotional distance, while symbols help you access the wisdom of the higher self. The first question however, is this: what tool(s) should you use if you don't already have a favorite method?

In choosing a divination system for yourself, think first about the sense to which you respond most strongly. Are you tactile? Visual? Your strongest sense gives you a good place to start in considering a divination system. For example, tactile people are often drawn to runes, crystals, or wooden slices with symbols thereon because of the feel of these items in the hand.

A very visual person is more than likely going to prefer a tarot deck, because it provides rich imagery. No matter what your sensual orientation is, take your time in finding a tool with symbols and sensations that really spark a strong positive reaction—those that seem to resonate with your spirit.

Now for those of you who feel that hearing, taste, or smell are your strongest primary senses, don't worry. You can use cues specific to your strongest sense during your divinatory efforts instead of using the sense itself in choosing a divination tool. For example, you could put on spiritually uplifting music, nibble on magickally prepared psychic foods, or burn incense that heightens awareness while using your chosen tool!

Once you have a tool that you enjoy using, you can pull it out when those difficult moments arise and you find your perspective wanting. One word of caution: Sometimes it's very hard to separate yourself from your hopes, fears, and wants. Try to see what your tool is really saying (not just what you *want* it to say, or what your mood is saying). To help overcome that possibility, you can smudge yourself with sage or cedar. This helps clean out your aura and any lingering energies that could influence the cards, stones, runes, or whatever you are using for a reading.

Throughout history, people have used all manner of divinatory tools, from charting the heavens to looking at tea leaves. Of the three most popular methods that our ancestors used—apples, numerology, and astrology—the latter two are still commonly practiced today.

Apple Magic

Apples were among the more quaint approaches to divination. Their use illustrates how people commonly used things in their living environment to lend perspectives on relationships. Why apples? Because they were reputed to be sacred to Venus, the goddess of love. Though it isn't commonly practiced anymore, you might want to give apple divination a try during the autumn, when apples are ripe and plentiful.

If you're hoping to meet a spouse in the not-too-distant future, peel the apple skin into one long strip. Toss that over your shoulder and then look at the peel as it sits. Whatever initial it forms is said to be one that your spouse will bear at the beginning of his or her first, middle, or last name.

Another interesting divination with apples includes a mirror. Just before midnight, take an apple and a candle and stand before a mirror (place the candle in front or to the side of the mirror to act as a divinatory focus). Eat the apple, tossing one piece over your right shoulder. Now, brush your hair. When the clock strikes midnight you should see the image of your future mate behind you in the mirror.

Numerology

If you aren't fond of having fruit parts on your floor, numerology offers a much cleaner alternative. The Greek philosopher Pythagoras was a great advocate of numerology. He felt that the entire universe could be explained and expressed in numbers—including our love lives. Simply stated, each personality can be boiled down to a correlative number, and that correlation helps us to see potentials (or the lack thereof) in terms of relationships.

Start with your date of birth and that of the potential or current partner. Each birth date needs to be reduced to one digit by adding up the digits. For example, if your birthday is January 16, 1965 (1/16/1965), you would reduce the date to one digit like this: 1+1+6+1+9+6+5 = 29; (2+9) = 11; (1+1) = 2. This is your birth number. Now do the same thing for your partner, and compare them based on the chart that follows.

Numerical relationships

1 and 1	Heated tempers due to very strong egos
1 and 2	A little old-fashioned, but relatively balanced
1 and 3	Very social; adventures on the horizon
1 and 4	Good communication skills needed—many fights

1 and 5	Huge in romance, but also very changeable
1 and 6	Financial stability and joy (but don't lose yourself)
1 and 7	Thinkers with periodic bursts of passion
1 and 8	Ambition runs high; watch your limits; set precedence
1 and 9	Differences and tantrums but physically WOW
2 and 2	A little too much alike many times
2 and 3	Patience, patience, patience; find mutual ground
2 and 4	Good long-term relationship, but rather bland
2 and 5	Love is strong, but your differences are likewise so
2 and 6	Very growth-oriented relationship for both
2 and 7	Good combination, but get out and socialize more
2 and 8	A balanced, yin-yang relationship
2 and 9	Uncertain; a relationship with huge mood swings
3 and 3	Good together, but a little too focused on risk-taking
3 and 4	Watch your money—both of you are spenders

3 and 5	Passionate and social people together
3 and 6	Happiness if you both stay proactive
3 and 7	Very different people—may or may not work
3 and 8	Opposites that attract, but can you make it?
3 and 9	Very dramatic relationship—love the spotlight
4 and 4	Earthy; well grounded but also inflexible
4 and 5	Very different personalities—iffy prospects
4 and 6	A solid relationship; express yourselves
4 and 7	Very solemn to the point of grimness
4 and 8	Long-term goals; strong work ethics
4 and 9	Not a good match
5 and 5	Green-eyed monster may overwhelm
5 and 6	Requires *lots* of give and take
5 and 7	Release each other to embrace love
5 and 8	Goal-oriented relationship
5 and 9	Adventurous; financially iffy
6 and 6	Demand perfection and giving
6 and 7	Difficult but possible
6 and 8	This relationship has fortitude
6 and 9	Normal and fairly content
7 and 7	Accept your human oddities; build respect
7 and 8	Work-oriented couple

7 and 9	Strong soul connection
8 and 8	Powerhouse (but need down time together)
8 and 9	Peace, symmetry; prioritize money
9 and 9	Deep friendship; long-term potential

As you can see, this is a very basic comparison of vibrations. Think of it as one ingredient in a much more complex recipe. Numerology can be far more complex than what's outlined above; on this level you're only getting a base resonance to which you must bring your own common sense and goals. If you have a really hot partner but your numbers are "off," then re-do the math by changing the way you handle this relationship!

For example, it's easy for the 8-8 relationship to become too focused on profit and the bottom line, while ignoring emotional issues. This happens because 8 (double four) is a strong earth-oriented number. With both of you having these goals, you need to periodically reconnect on a heart level, and let your minds rest!

Astrology

The pickup line from the 1960s ("what's your sign, baby?") has become a bit of a joke, but the fact that we all still laugh about it says something about how astrology has affected the way we think about life and our relationships. At least 20 percent of Americans surveyed in 2003 believe in astrology, and well over 40 percent say they read an astrology column regularly. This certainly mirrors the old aphorism: It's all in the stars!

As with numerology, astrology can get very complex, very quickly. The following are some general guidelines that you can use in grooming a relationship, at least superficially. For example, if you know you're with someone who astrologically isn't the ideal, find aspects of that sign's personality that really light your fire, or that you admire. Focus on those and work on the rest!

Astro Compatability Chart

Aries—Leo, Sagittarius, Gemini, and Aquarius

Taurus—Virgo, Capricorn, Cancer, and Pisces

Gemini—Libra, Aquarius, Aries, and Leo

Cancer—Scorpio, Pisces, Taurus, and Virgo

Leo—Aries, Sagittarius, Gemini, and Libra

Virgo—Taurus, Capricorn, Cancer, and Scorpio

Libra—Gemini, Aquarius, Leo, and Sagittarius

Scorpio—Cancer, Pisces, Virgo, and Capricorn

Sagittarius—Leo, Aries, Libra, and Aquarius

Capricorn—Virgo, Taurus, Scorpio, and Pisces

Aquarius—Libra, Gemini, Sagittarius, and Aries

Pisces—Scorpio, Cancer, Capricorn, and Taurus

Basic compatibility aside, what can you expect from a lover based on his or her birth sign? Well, if you're dating or intimate with an Aries, you can anticipate that this person is going to be a bit like a push-me-pull-you (meaning they like to tease!). Aries is typically passionate, sometimes even aggressively so. Take your vitamins, as they expect you to keep up! As a kisser, Aries will sneak up and kiss you deeply, then run off to play without a second thought. Keep your sneakers on!

Taurus is every bit as strong and steady as you'd imagine from a bull. Embracing a sense of style without leaving behind a desire for secure foundations, Taurus lovers try to get what they want, but always with personal flair and charm. That doesn't mean they leave their mates behind in a blur of personal goals, however—your needs are important to them too, and they can be very romantic and incredibly long lasting! Similarly, the kiss from your Taurus lover will last forever (and this sign finds it quite a turn-on!).

Gemini, by comparison, is as curious and excited as a seven-year-old at a state fair. Their attention will seem to be everywhere, and they never stop talking. This personality can be both funny and fun, but also requires a lot of flexibility as you never know which twin you're talking to from one minute to the next! Look for a lot of fire and energy in the bedroom (warning—I mean a *lot*). As a kisser Gemini can be frustrating because they get distracted easily. However, if you're looking for unique sexual encounters, this partner will more than likely welcome a challenge!

Moving to Cancer, here you have the ultimate homebody-family person. They love being in their personal space, preferably a home that's truly "theirs." You'll find that a Cancer lover will always want to take you to his or her place, but because of a strong water-based nature filled with emotions, the sex can run hot and cold. As a kisser, Cancer will be warm and wonderful when their emotions are "on."

While Cancer is on an emotional ebb and flow, Leo is busy speaking his or her mind—loudly, frequently, and whether or not anyone wants to hear. This pussycat talks a good talk, and if you want someone to tell you a steamy "bedtime story," Leo is a great choice. You'll get the best results in bed when you compliment Leo, play with their mane, or put on a fantasy kitty-cat costume. As for kissing, expect the unexpected from this wild child (watch out, lions may bite!).

Your Virgo lover might require a little persistent coaxing to come out of his or her shell. Virgos tend toward shyness. However, if you need a lover or mate who can organize anything, this is a good sign to consider. Better still, Virgos can talk nearly as well as they can manage, often being the diplomats in any given situation. Do not expect an exciting kisser here—the gesture is often so light and fleeting that it's barely noticeable.

The Libra mate wants balance. He or she has tons of charm and grace, but also needs to hear about those attributes from time to time to stay on an even emotional keel. And should you betray a Libra lover—beware! When they love, they love fully . . . but when they're angry they have incredibly long memories, and the determination and wherewithal to "get even." As a kisser, Libra typically isn't overly interested—they're more turned on by shopping.

Scorpios have a lot of raw energy that can be channeled into your erotic moments. The only problem is that Scorpio's fiery nature can be a bit overwhelming. There's more than enough sexual interest here for two or three lovers, accompanied by an equal number of emotional hurdles to get through before reaching a trusting level. You might as well give up ever trying to keep a secret from this person—they want things out in the open. As to kissing? Why bother? Let's just get to the sex!

A Sagittarius lover will be inquisitive and curious, even a bit adventurous if he or she feels that something new will please and tease you. Because this sign is ever philosophical and flirtatious, talking is integral to all Sagittarian relationships (be ready to listen a lot). Additionally, the Sagittarius man or woman is staunchly independent and self-sufficient. Whiny, clingy people and drama kings or queens need not apply! As a kisser, the Sagittarians always leave their lovers wanting more.

Capricorns, meanwhile, are busy trying to create the "perfect" romance (even if there is no such thing to be found). Idealistically, they try new and interesting ways to please their lovers—the flashier and more surprising, the better. Capricorns typically seek out people who can be effective partners in and out of the bedroom, because they want to enjoy their lovers in all parts of life! Capricorns find kissing very relaxing, to the point of maybe taking a nap, so leave that for after-sex snuggling.

The Aquarius in your life is a magnetic and curious creature. He or she wants friendship and caring just as much as passion, perhaps more so. In fact, some sense of stability is very healthy to the Aquarian sex drive (they don't want to worry who they'll be waking up next to). To appeal to his or her body, appeal to the Aquarian mind first. Think, live, laugh, and love outside of what society considers the "norm." As a kisser—watch out for a watery wet one!

Finally, the Pisces lover is insightful, whimsical, gentle, and intuitive, but also can keep a secret better than most vaults! They love to spring surprises, from an unexpected gift to a naughty little nightgown. Just be aware that the fish swim in highly emotional waters. They love deeply and live very fully, but also get hurt easily. The Piscean loves to kiss dreamily, thoughtfully, and typically it's quite a turn-on.

Rituals of Romance

There are a lot of rituals in various world traditions that focus on matters of the heart, marriage being a very familiar one. But what if you and your partner want to use ritual in different ways—in ways that help connect you more intimately, inspire more passion, or that further mutual goals through magick? This chapter provides help, hints, and examples for creating a sacred space ideal for magickal lovemaking.

Marriage and Conception Rituals

The two most common times that a couple enacts a special sensual ritual are after a wedding and when they wish to have children. In the first case, the couple invokes a special type of blessing to deepen their intimacy, and complete the circle of their union by being as close as two people can possibly get. In the second case, a couple seeks to use sacred space to empower their goal of having a child, born out of mutual love. Let's consider the honeymoon ritual first.

The Sacred We

When a couple gets married, it doesn't just change their tax status. There's a distinct shift in each person's auric field that makes a space for each other. That space becomes a spot where the energies of both people mingle freely together—the Sacred We. How well those vibrations mix, dance, and play together indicates the level of successful intimacy two people have with each other.

Mind you, all relationships take time and effort. The pre-wedding preparations and any special magick you work during your honeymoon is only one step in ongoing relationship maintenance. Even so, it's a wonderful way to set the tone for your relationship and all that's to come in the future.

If you are about to be married, create a little charm that somehow represents your hopes and wishes for your marriage, or perhaps what you feel you are personally bringing to the relationship. Do not tell your partner what you've made. For example, one individual I knew made a clay hammer as his token. He was a carpenter, and the hammer represented his desire to use his abilities to create strong foundations for himself and his wife. His wife, on the other hand, created a broom to sweep out things from the past that neither of them wanted or needed in their new relationship. She made the broom from homegrown lavender (for peace) and blessed it beneath the light of a full moon for three nights before the wedding.

In this couple's case, they used the tokens as part of the wedding ritual. Each presented the token at the exchange of vows and left those items on the marriage altar. If you are not able to do this or prefer to keep your tokens for a more private moment, use these charms as part of your honeymoon ritual instead. You may also want to consider making or finding smaller tokens that you and your partner can always carry with you so that you can take the magick of love with you wherever you may go.

Some other things you'll want to think about having for the honeymoon ritual include incense (perhaps rose for romance), statuary (if you want to honor a deity and invite that Being's blessings into the space), music, and playful clothing. Each item chosen should be as meaningful as possible to both of you, and mirror your goals of unity, happiness, harmony, or whatever else is important to you. One nice touch is that of having three candles for the altar, one for each of you, and one that represents your combined energies—the Sacred We. If you think of this ritual as a sacred and wholly personalized play in which the two of you create the set, the story, and the ending, you'll do just fine!

Note: If you are honeymooning out of the country, review the restrictions on plant matter and other items that you may want to take across international borders before you make decisions about this part of the ritual. You don't want to have a fuss with customs (it really puts the kibosh on the whole mood you're trying to create). No matter your destination, put all of the items for your ritual together in a safe spot so they won't get accidentally left behind.

When you arrive at the ritual destination (probably wherever you're honeymooning), feel out your surroundings. What do you feel you want to add or put away so that you have the perfect ambiance? This might be the ideal time to consider creating sacred space and putting out your do-not-disturb sign!

Any flat surface can become your altar. If you find that the religious connotations of an altar make you uncomfortable, simply think of it as a central location at which you're going to celebrate and honor your relationship in a special way. Put your tokens on the surface, along with anything else you feel is meaningful, such as candles.

Change into the clothing you want to wear. Lightly mist the room with your personal perfumes or colognes so that the energy of the space is keyed to the two of you. Light the personal candles and stand hand-in-hand before your tokens. If you're going to invite the Divine to bless your union or share in this moment, a simple shared prayer is one way of so doing. Just speak from your heart of your dreams and hopes and all that you're feeling. Finally, explain the meaning of your token to your mate, and let him or her do likewise.

At this point, light the union candle (make sure that you place it somewhere safe so it can continue to burn brightly, like your love), and let your passion and love guide you. Our magickal, spiritual nature has a way of helping us even when we feel a little nervous. While enacting this ritual does take a bit of planning, it's well worth your time. You'll find that adding a little magick to your honeymoon night adds a level of intimacy and bonding that you may not have otherwise experienced.

And Baby Makes Three: Conception Ritual

Some couples blend this ritual into their honeymoon night, but typically it's better to work conception magick when the moon is full, when the woman is fertile, and when you can completely focus on that goal.

Before talking about designing the ritual itself, let's consider some pragmatics. When you're thinking about a child, there are a lot of elements that make up the equation, including personal time, living space, and all the changes that a baby will bring to the dynamics of your relationship. Responsible magick means that you consider the practicalities first so that there's no uncertainty or misgivings to hinder the flow of energy.

Next, talk over the idea of a ritual with your partner. Establish a common vision so that you can create the ritual together. Most often, you'll want to enact the ritual very shortly before lovemaking; however, sex should not be the whole focus of this event. For one thing, it puts way too much pressure on you and your partner to "perform." Making a baby is a loving action, not a command performance! So rather than stressing the sexual aspect, consider directing your thoughts and energies toward your partner and toward the spirit of the child with whom you hope to share your life.

As with the honeymoon ritual, ponder aromatics, imagery, and other sensual cues that mirror your goals. Some of the aromatics used for fertility include musk and vervain. For imagery, a collage of baby pictures from magazines is one suggestion, as is a newly budding plant, or a statue of a pregnant goddess. Around the loving space, use a lot of pale yellow highlights for creative energy, and if you're feeling whimsical, put a paper stork over the bed! Creating an atmosphere of laughter and joy is an excellent way to welcome the energies of a child into your life.

Making a fertility token is also a nice touch for this event. You can put together charms for each other that are intended to improve virility and pleasure. Nuts and seeds are two things that have historically been used in fertility charms, because they speak of the earth's fertility and abundance. If you'd like to use those, take a piece of natural yellow cloth and wrap the chosen seeds or nuts within. Add an incantation like this one:

Between me and thee, let there be
The blessing of fertility.

Tie the cloth with a piece of yarn three times (three, in this case, represents you, your mate, and the child you hope to have). Carry the charm with you for a minimum of three days before your ritual. Three represents the mind, body, and soul working in harmony. Four days of carrying the tokens creates strong foundations in which that harmony grows, and five days brings to it that spark of magick! However, as with any other magickal process, utilize a number of days that is functional for your circumstances and meaningful to the two of you.

On your conception altar, place a symbol for each of you, for the family, and for the yet-to-be child. I like using a white birthday candle for the child's spirit. A yoni (vaginal) and phallic symbol are also apt here. You can light the personal and family candles at the outset of your ritual, and light the child's candle after lovemaking for improved symbolic impact.

Cleansing, ritual bathing, and anointing can also help put you and your partner in the right frame of mind. These small actions help us make the transition from the mundane to the magickal. It also provides you both with a time of pampering, which helps everyone relax.

Cleansing and anointing create a very intimate touch. Use the tub or the shower. Surround the area with candles, burn a little incense, play the music you've chosen, and then give your partner an inspiring natural sponge bath. You and your partner can visualize any unwanted energies being washed away during this time, and you can also project the type of vibrations into your hands (and the sponge) that both of you hope to create.

Don't forget to be playful if the muse so inspires! While sacredness has a serious side, relationships as a whole benefit from humor and fun. The gods and goddesses love a smile!

The next step is creating sacred space, if you wish. It's not necessary to conception, but it does make the energy around your lovemaking a little more special. If you decide to do this, find words that reflect your goals and the intimate nature of the space you're creating. You may wish to start the invocation in the south (to honor the fires of love or passion), and then dismiss starting in the west (to cool the fires, and honor our emotions). Here's an example:

> *Powers of the south—of fire and passion*
> *Come and watch over this sacred space*
> *Inspire us with your sparks; ignite our spirits*
>   *with light*
> *Open the way for the child of our love.*
> *Powers of the west—of water and emotion*
> *Come watch over this sacred space*
> *Inspire us with insight; wash us with unity*
> *Open the way for the child of our hearts.*
> *Powers of the north—of earth and growth*
> *Come watch over this sacred space*
> *Inspire us with foundations, give our magick rich soil*
>   *in which to grow*
> *Open the way for the child of our bodies.*
> *Powers of the east—of air and communication*
> *Come watch over this sacred space*
> *Inspire us with transformation, move among us with*
>   *the breath of life*
> *Open the way for the child of our wishes and dreams*
> *So be it.*

At this juncture, start breathing in unison. Don't force this. Take a nice deep breath in through your nose, out through your mouth, and then take each other's hands. Continue breathing in the same manner while paying attention to the pace of your partner. Within about five minutes, you should find yourselves in sync.

This is when inspired loving begins. You and your partner should continue to focus on the goal of welcoming a child into your life, and allow the cone of power to naturally grow until climax, where it's released to that need/goal.

These are just two examples of ways to deepen your spiritual rapport with your partner while likewise expanding your relationship in wonderful and meaningful ways. No matter the goal, no matter the timing, you and your partner are sacred, and your bodies are sacred and sensual. Celebrate that, honor it, and enjoy it fully!

*let me tell you, that the more the pleasures
of the body fade away, the greater to me is
the pleasure and charm of conversation.*

plato

Afterword:
Pillow Talk

celebrating the sensual you

t the end of the day, sensuality and pleasure very frequently boil down to about how you feel about yourself, how you feel about your partner(s), and how you express both in your reality. Many of us have spent months or years feeling insecure, ugly, passionless, or uninteresting. This is a fallacy perpetuated by a society that's lost sight of the Sacred Self—that shining, vibrant person that lives in every soul.

If you get nothing else from this book, my prayer is that from this moment forward you will embrace sacred sensuality and sexuality as something you *own*. It doesn't come from outside; it can't be manipulated by surgery; it won't suddenly happen after you've had X number of lovers—you must trust in it, *be* it. Look in the mirror, but see the true you: the person who dares to live, love, and laugh fully—the sensual sorceress who is primed for magick and merrymaking. It is your birthright, and more important, it's something you owe yourself. You deserve rich happiness in all aspects of your life. Grab hold of that happiness and celebrate the sensual, sacred You today.